Communication Skills in the New Millennium

Y0-BPW-110

Standardized
Test Preparation

Level I

BARRETT KENDALL PUBLISHING

AUSTIN, TEXAS

ISBN 1-58079-344-4

1 2 3 4 5 6 7   HG   06 05 04 03 02 01 00

Table of Contents

Introduction

The Standardized Test Preparation component of *BK English* has been developed in order to provide today's classroom teacher with an easy way to incorporate test preparation into daily instruction. Studies show that when students understand how they arrive at an answer to a test question, they perform better on tests. Similarly, test prep that incorporates the content of day-to-day instruction is more engaging and effective. Our goal in creating this book is to help you teach students to incorporate test-taking strategies and critical thinking skills into their daily learning, no matter what their individual learning styles and levels of ability and interest may be.

This book will help prepare students for standardized tests in reading and writing. The reading passages, comprehension questions, writing prompts, and editing questions included in this book match the format on most such standardized tests. What distinguishes this book from most test preparation is its *thematic* content. Each of the 15 thematic units in this book is designed to help you incorporate test-taking practice into the material you teach. The teaching suggestions at the beginning of each unit can help prompt discussion. In addition, you may want to bring in literature or other reading materials related to the themes presented in this book. Note that the themes are carefully chosen to tie in to the instruction you may be giving in Composition or other subject areas.

Because students are often faced with so much pressure and repetition in studying for tests, these reading and writing exercises are intended to grab students' interest with a rich variety of subjects related to issues in students' lives. The reading selections provide students with knowledge in the subject, which can be reinforced first through the follow-up discussion and then through the writing prompt, which encourages students to incorporate prior knowledge with what they learn from the reading selection to produce a composition.

EACH UNIT CONTAINS THE FOLLOWING:

- **Lesson preparation suggestions** for the teacher, including questions to help stimulate classroom discussion of the topic of the unit, an overview of the skills covered by the unit, and suggestions for how to make the most of the material

READING

- **Fiction and/or nonfiction reading passages** on the unit topic that vary in length in order to give the student a range of reading experiences
- **Six multiple-choice questions** per reading passage testing comprehension and critical reading skills

COMPOSITION

- **An engaging and stimulating writing prompt** related to the reading passage, intended to help the student relate the reading to his or her own experience
- **A graphic organizer for each writing prompt** to help today's visually oriented student in prewriting and developing ideas for the writing exercise

LANGUAGE

- **A paragraph-form editing exercise** with multiple-choice questions testing skills in grammar, usage, and mechanics

TEACHER'S SUGGESTIONS

DISCUSSION QUESTIONS

The focus of this unit is North American bears, their habitat, and their interaction with humans. To encourage discussion of the topic, share the following information with students:

- Grizzly bears used to roam over most of Alaska, Canada, and the continental United States. Today, they have been exterminated almost completely from the 48 continuous states and occupy 1% of their former territory. How do you feel about removing animals from their natural habitats now populated by humans?

- Some naturalists say that encountering a bear in the wild is more of a privilege than a hazard. Why would seeing a wild animal in its natural habitat be considered a "privilege"?

- President Clinton proposed that the federal government double the amount of money that it spent on land acquisition for national parks. Many congressmen opposed this proposal, arguing that the federal government had too much land already. How do you feel about spending federal money on increasing the national park system? Do you think the government has too much land?

READING—*Identifying Main Ideas*

- Ask students to make a list of the main idea in each paragraph and the supporting ideas in each paragraph in the articles. Using a word-web graphic organizer, list the main idea with the supporting ideas surrounding it.

- Encourage students to brainstorm their own ideas about bears and animals using the same type of organizer.

COMPOSITION—*Strengthening Arguments*

- Have students brainstorm a list of some positive attributes of national parks. Working in small groups, have them devise ad campaigns promoting parks using the items on their list.

- Have students suppose that a black bear has been discovered living in their city or town. Ask them to write letters to the mayor explaining why the bear should be allowed to stay or not.

EDITING—*Review Punctuation and Capitalization Rules*

- Use commas to separate two clauses in a compound sentence.
  - **EXAMPLE** "Grizzly bears used to roam over much of Northern America, but now they have been mostly exterminated."

- Use a comma to separate the elements in a series.
  - **EXAMPLE** "She collects stuffed koalas, pandas, polar, and brown bears."

- Capitalize the first word in a sentence, proper nouns, and the pronoun *I*.
  - **EXAMPLE** "You can tell Mary to forget about camping in North America now!" I cried.

▶ **READING**

Read the passages "What to Do in Bear Country," "Frenzied Grizzly Kills Hiker," and "The Sad Fate of a Mother Grizzly," and answer the questions that follow.

WHAT TO DO IN BEAR COUNTRY

If you are ever camping in bear country, it may be useful for you to know that most bears want to avoid you as much as you want to avoid them. Unlike the stereotype of bears as vicious man-eating beasts, bears are actually quite shy around humans. They know that humans are their only predators and, quite prudently, choose to avoid them rather than risk trouble.

Like most animals in the wild, bears like to eat the most nutritious foods around that are the least difficult to get. Berries, nuts, insects, honey, and grasses are just some of the foods they consume. Contrary to popular belief (and the Yogi Bear cartoon), most bears prefer food found in the wild to human food. It is only when resources are scarce, like during periods of intense heat or drought, that a bear will try to eat human food.

Because they have such a wide habitat range and are so numerous, black bears are the bears that people most encounter. There are approximately 400,000 to 750,000 black bears in North America. Their range extends from the southern edge of the Arctic through most of Canada and the United States, all the way to the northwest mountains of the Sierra Madres in Mexico.

If you are hiking or camping in bear country, here are some tips on what to do:

- **Make a lot of noise.** Bears will normally avoid interaction with humans. Be sure to make noise as you hike or camp to let bears know you are there. Attacks usually happen when someone gets between a sow and her cubs, surprises a bear, or gets between a bear and its food.
- **Stay your ground, wave your arms and talk to the bear.** If you encounter a bear in the wild, stay calm and resist the impulse to run. Bears, like all animals, can sense fear and know that a frightened being is dangerous and unpredictable. Instead, wave your arms and talk to (rather than shout at) the bear. The bear will see that you are not a threat and will usually walk away.
- **Keep a clean camp.** Be sure to put all food and garbage in a bag tied to a rope and thrown high up (twelve to fifteen feet), over a tree branch, away from the trunk. Never keep your food in your tent with you at night, or even in your car, for that matter. Hungry bears have been known to bend open car doors and break through windshields in order to get to food.
- **Learn about the area you are traveling in.** Contact local park rangers or the Wildlife Refuge before making a trip in bear country. Seeing a bear in the wild is a privilege few encounter. The more you know what to expect, the better off both you and the bears will be.

FRENZIED GRIZZLY KILLS HIKER

A hiker was attacked and eaten at Glacier Park, Montana by a ferocious mother grizzly bear. No one knows for certain why the bear attacked and killed, as the hiker had no food in his backpack. Rangers suspect that the man surprised the bear or came between the sow and her cubs. His mauled body was discovered by another backcountry climber after she noticed a pair of glasses lying in a pool of blood near the trail.

"I was scared," the hiker, Laura Trimly of Hoboken, New Jersey, admitted. "I didn't know if the bear was still around. I didn't know what to do. I just wanted to get out of there but I had to see if someone was still alive, if someone needed my help."

Not far from the trail she discovered what appeared to be the remains of a human body. "That was enough for me," she recalled. " I had to warn other hikers and get help."

When rangers arrived on the scene two hours later, the body was no longer where Ms. Trimly had indicated it would be. Cautiously, ever aware of the danger and the possibility that they may be attacked themselves, the rangers followed the tracks on the trail where it was clear the body had been dragged. Five hundred yards down a heavily wooded slope, the rangers discovered the torn remains of David Mander, a furniture dealer from Pittsburgh, Pennsylvania.

THE SAD FATE OF A MOTHER GRIZZLY

A grizzly guilty only of protecting her cubs was hunted and killed by rangers in Glacier Park, Montana. Mere hours after the mother bear had attacked a solitary hiker in order to protect her young from harm, rangers determined the bear must die.

"It was a hard decision," Ranger Bob Conner declared. "In most cases, a bear will neutralize a threat and then leave. It is extremely rare that a bear will actually attack humans in this predatory manner." It was the fact that the bear had eaten parts of the man that led the rangers to believe that the bear should be killed.

"By removing this one bear we perhaps saved many bears," Conner claimed. If the bear had been allowed to live, he asserted, any attack that occurred in the park after that would have been because of the "man-killing grizzly" in the public eye and would have meant more trouble for grizzlies in the long run.

"We want an atmosphere where people and bears can coexist," he said. But having a bear in the park that has found food by eating a person is not what the park has in mind. "It was awful to shoot that bear," stated Conner, "but it was the right thing to do."

UNIT 1

____ **1.** What definition most closely conveys the meaning of the word "prudently" in the following sentence? They know that humans are their only predators and, quite prudently, choose to avoid them rather than risk trouble.

A behaving rashly

B exercising good judgement

C careful about one's appearance

D shy around strangers

____ **2.** Which one of the following best describes the main idea of "What to Do in Bear Country"?

A Bears are dangerous wild animals that should be avoided.

B Bears eat berries, nuts, and insects because they are nutritious.

C Keep a food in a tree when camping in bear country.

D Learn what to expect from bears before hiking or camping in bear country.

____ **3.** Which one of the following best summarizes "Frenzied Grizzly Kills Hiker"?

A A dangerous bear randomly attacks a loan hiker.

B A brave woman finds a dead body.

C Rangers use caution when following bear tracks.

D Hikers' need better gear when walking in bear country.

____ **4.** Black bears are the bears that people encounter the most because—

A they are numerous and live in highly populated areas

B they are cute and easily approachable

C they have a wide habitat range and there are many of them

D they are aggressive and attack hikers

____ **5.** If you encounter a bear and wave your arms and talk to it, it will probably—

A attack you

B go away

C eat your food

D sense fear

____ **6.** Which one of the following statements expresses a fact?

A Black bears are wild animals that usually attack humans.

B Bears prefer to eat foods that are nutritious and easy to obtain.

C Bears are cuddly and will eat your food if you let them.

D Bears are scary and should be kept out of national parks.

7. After reading the article "What to do in Bear Country," do you think people should be allowed to hike in bear country? Explain your position.

_____
_____
_____
_____
_____
_____

8. What are the arguments presented in "Frenzied Grizzly Kills Hiker" and "The Sad Fate of a Mother Grizzly"? Discuss the main points and how they use the same evidence to come up with different conclusions.

_____
_____
_____
_____
_____

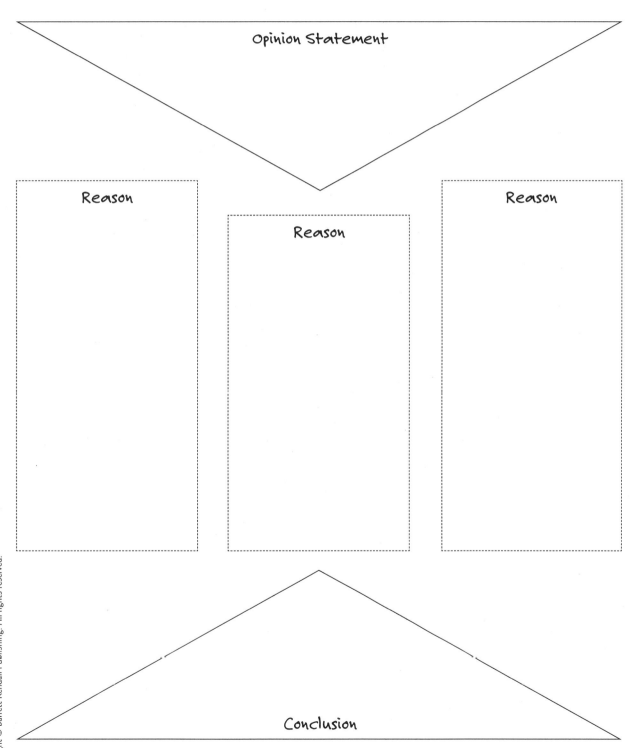

COMPOSITION

Imagine that you are an editor for your local newspaper. Recently there has been some public debate about whether or not more land in the United States should be turned into national parks. What do you think? Write an editorial for the local newspaper persuading your readers to support your position. Be sure to use facts and examples to support your opinions, and be sure to organize your details in a logical order.

Use the graphic organizer below to organize your ideas.

Opinion Statement

Reason

Reason

Reason

Conclusion

EDITING

Read the following passage and determine which type of error, if any, appears in the underlined section. Write the letter of the correct answer.

....

In Scandinavia <u>durring the Viking period</u> many people believed that certain
(1)
individuals had the ability to change into or assume the characteristics of bears.

They thought that if a warrior put on a bear-skin shirt (called a *bear-sark*),

<u>which had been treated with oils and herbs then that</u> warrior would become as
(2)
strong and powerful as a bear. <u>During battle, the warrior, would become frenzied,</u>
(3)
able to bite through his enemy's shields or walk through a fire without burning

himself. In <u>Modern English, the word *berserk* comes from this scandinavian myth.</u>
(4)

____ **1. A** Spelling error
    B Capitalization error
    C Punctuation error
    D No error

____ **2. A** Spelling error
    B Capitalization error
    C Punctuation error
    D No error

____ **3. A** Spelling error
    B Capitalization error
    C Punctuation error
    D No error

____ **4. A** Spelling error
    B Capitalization error
    C Punctuation error
    D No error

DISCUSSION QUESTIONS

The focus of this unit is Sherman Alexie's short story "This is What it Means to Say Phoenix, Arizona." To encourage discussion of the topic, ask the following questions:

- Sherman Alexie has said that when he was a boy he never dreamed of being a writer or filmmaker, because "Growing up on a reservation, nobody tells you that you can do this." What do you think of this statement? Do you feel you can grow up and do anything? Why or why not?

- In the story, the two boys are not friends and know that even after the intimate experience or their journey they will still not be friends. Have you ever experienced anything like this? What was it like?

- Alexie has said that as an Indian writer he is often taken to be a spokesperson for all things American Indian. Why do you think he might feel this way?

READING—*Analyzing Structures*

- Ask students to break down the information given in the article into a list.

- Encourage students to combine the information on their list in different orders. How would changing the order of the information affect the reader's understanding of the article?

COMPOSITION—*Responding Appropriately in a Written Composition*

- Break your class into groups. Have each group brainstorm a list of characteristics that best represents their culture either as an American or another culture that unites the group. Then have each group share their list with the class.

- Ask students to freewrite about one of the characteristics from their lists.

- Have students write an essay describing the meaning of their characteristic as it relates to their culture and/or being an American.

EDITING—*Using Conjunctions*

Remind students that conjunctions are used to express a connection between words. The most familiar conjunctions are *and*, *but*, and *or*, which are **coordinators** (connecting elements of equal syntactic status).

> **EXAMPLE** Fred *and* Mary play bingo.

Subordinators are conjunctions that connect elements of unequal syntactic status. They include *if, although, because, before, since, till, unless, whereas* and *whether*.

> **EXAMPLE** Fred will play bingo *if* Mary will join him.

▷ **READING**

Read the passage "Sherman Alexie's 'This Is What It Means to Say Phoenix, Arizona'," and answer the questions that follow.

··

SHERMAN ALEXIE'S "THIS IS WHAT IT MEANS TO SAY PHOENIX, ARIZONA"

Sherman Alexie's "This is What It Means to Say Phoenix, Arizona" is the story of two not-quite-friends who take a road trip from their Indian Reservation in Washington all the way to a trailer park in Phoenix, Arizona. The story encompasses more than the average road trip, coming-of-age narrative, however. With his bleak, ironic humor and lyric style, Alexie weaves a tale of growing up, finding one's identity, being a member of a community, and making peace with the past while learning to embrace the future. He also challenges the traditional image of two Native American archetypes— the warrior and the shaman.

The story opens with Victor learning that his father, whom he has not seen in years, has died in a trailer in Phoenix. Victor has just lost his job and doesn't have the money to get to Arizona. ("Who does have money on a reservation," the narrator asks, "except the cigarette and fireworks salespeople?") Victor runs into Thomas-Builds-the-Fire, a storyteller "that nobody wanted to listen to. That's like being a dentist in a town where everybody has false teeth." Victor and Thomas have known each other their whole lives, yet are not friends. Thomas is an outsider, a misfit, while Victor is "cool"—his friends would laugh at him for spending time with Thomas. Thomas, however, has enough money to help Victor get to Phoenix, on the condition that he will take Thomas with him. Victor agrees, and the two set off on their journey.

The contrast of the story's ironic tone with Thomas' flights of lyricism serves to create a darkly realistic world. In the course of the story, the reader learns that Victor's father was an alcoholic who abandoned the family and Thomas-Build-the-Fire is an orphan with only his stories for company. Yet the two share more in common than they realize. They are both part of the same tribe. They both long to be warriors. They both struggle to discover the place where their Indian community fits into the larger American context.

"I remember I had this dream that told me to go to Spokane," Thomas tells Victor, ". . . your Dad came walking up. What . . . are you doing here? he asked me. I said, Waiting for a vision. Then your father said, All you're going to do here is get mugged. So he drove me over to Denny's, bought me dinner, and drove me home to the reservation. For a long time I was mad because I thought my dreams had lied to me. But they didn't. Your dad was my vision. Take care of each other is what my dreams were saying. Take care of each other."

In the character of Thomas-Builds-the-Fire, Alexie has created an anomaly: the Indian seer as a nerd who is shunned, rather than respected, by his tribe. In Victor, he has written a warrior whose enemies are intangibles—poverty and despair—rather than human. In this way, Alexie challenges romanticized notions of Native Americans and places his story firmly in the present. His are modern characters, dealing with modern problems, but from the perspective of a pre-modern culture. "An Indian's whole life is guided, shaped and controlled by memory, in a much more tangible way than for most Americans." Alexie says. And the power of memories to both heal and hurt is evident throughout the story.

Ultimately, however, it is the human capacity to surprise that resonates from the ironic humor of the story—the surprise of two people helping each other and being generous with each other when it is not their first impulse. This generosity of spirit is unexpected and bittersweet, affecting both character and reader alike.

_____ **1.** The word <u>anomaly</u> in the fifth paragraph means
  A deviation from the rule
  B catastrophe
  C error
  D mistake

_____ **2.** One of the ways in which Alexie challenges romantic notions of American Indians in the story is by—
  A writing about two boys
  B writing characters who are guided by memories
  C having Thomas mention his vision
  D creating a warrior character whose enemies are poverty and despair

_____ **3.** Which sentence do you think best describes the theme of "This Is What It Means to Say Phoenix, Arizona"?
  A Members of a community are more connected than they realize and need to look out for and help one another.
  B Alcoholism is damaging and can ruin relationships.
  C "Cool" people should never socialize with "nerds."
  D Indians in America have a hard time living on reservations.

_____ **4.** Victor agrees to take Thomas with him because—
  A he feels guilty that he was not kind to Thomas in the past
  B he wants Thomas to share the driving
  C Thomas offers to help Victor pay for the trip
  D Victor is depressed

_____ **5.** The fact that both Victor and Thomas were raised on a reservation and are American Indian is—
  A essential to the story
  B a minor detail to the story
  C hardly mentioned in the story
  D not relevant to the characters story

_____ **6.** Which one of the following statements expresses an opinion?
  A Victor's father was an alcoholic who left his family.
  B Thomas-Builds-the-Fire is considered an outsider.
  C Sherman Alexie is the greatest living American Indian writer.
  D Sherman Alexie uses humor to tell his story.

7. After reading the passage, how do you think Alexie challenges traditional images of American Indians? Explain your position.

  _____
  _____
  _____
  _____
  _____

▶ COMPOSITION

Sherman Alexie has stated in interviews that the first time he ever read an anthology of Native American literature, he saw his life in poems and stories for the very first time and thought, "Somebody understands me!" Have you ever had the experience of recognizing yourself in a piece of fiction or poetry? Write a short essay for your class describing what it was like, if you have, or what has been missing, if you have not.

Use the following word-web to help organize your thoughts.

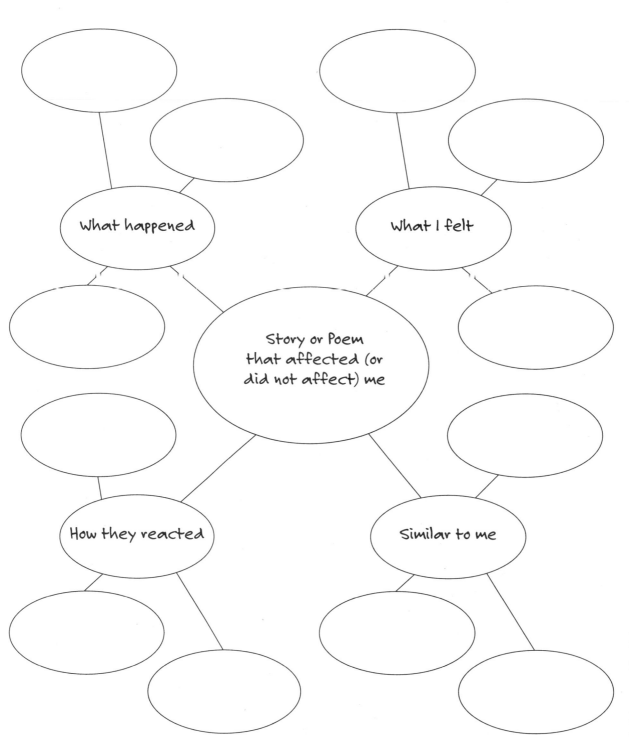

EDITING

Read the following. The underlined sections may be one of the following:
- **Run-on sentence**
- **Correctly written sentences that should be combined**
- **Correctly written sentences that do not need to be re-written**

Choose the best way to write each underlined section and mark the letter for your answer. If the sentence needs no change, mark "Correct as is."

Sherman Alexie planned on being a doctor when he first attended <u>college he</u>

<u>fainted three times in his anatomy class and figured that he "needed a career change."</u>
                                    (1)

<u>Only one course was available. A poetry writing workshop.</u> It was there that
                                    (2)

Alexie discovered poems and stories written by First Nations people. <u>He had an</u>

<u>epiphany, he realized he wanted to be a writer.</u> Since that day, <u>Alexie has published</u>
                    (3)   **(4)**

<u>novels, poetry, and even a screenplay.</u>

____ **1. A** collcgc. Oncc thcrc, hc faintcd three times in his anatomy class and figured that he "needed a career change."

B college, he fainted three times in his anatomy class and figured that he "needed a career change."

C college; he fainted three times in his anatomy class and figured that he "needed a career change."

D Correct as is

____ **2. A** Only one course was available. The poetry writing workshop.

B Only one course was available, being a poetry writing workshop.

C Only one course, a poetry writing workshop, was available.

D Correct as is

____ **3. A** IIe had an epiphany. Realizing he wanted to be a writer.

B He had an epiphany, realizing he wanted to be a writer.

C He had an epiphany, realized he wanted to be a writer.

D Correct as is

____ **4. A** Alexie has published novels. Poetry and a screenplay.

B Alexie has published novels— poetry and a screenplay.

C Alexie has published novels, poetry, screenplay.

D Correct as is

DISCUSSION QUESTIONS

The focus of this unit is the history and habitat of the giant squid. To encourage discussion of the topic, ask the following questions:

- What would it be like to see a giant squid? How do you think you would feel?
- What might scientists learn by observing a giant squid in its natural habitat?

READING—*Recognizing Points of View*

As students read the passage, ask them to think about the following questions.

- Is the primary intent of the author of this article to inform, to persuade, to express, or to entertain?
- What clues are there in the article which show the author's intent?
- How does the author's perspective affect the text?

COMPOSITION—*Refining Style to Suit Occasion, Audience, and Purpose*

Play a piece of evocative classical music. Ask students to image that this music is the soundtrack to a movie featuring giant squids.

- Have students freewrite for five minutes about the action that accompanies the soundtrack.
- Have students share their freewriting with the class.
- Ask students to pick an idea from their own or someone else's freewriting and have them freewrite for an additional five minutes.

EDITING—*Using Semicolons*

Remind students about semicolon use with the following:

- A semicolon is used to separate the items in a list after a colon.
    EXAMPLE The following books make references to giant squid: Homer's *Odyssey*; Jules Verne's *20,000 Under the Sea*; and Richard Ellis' *Monsters From the Sea*.
- A semicolon is also used to separate two independent clauses in one sentence.
    EXAMPLE "Giant squid may hunt whales; it is hard to be certain, though."

A simple test is this: if you can use a period and a new sentence, you can use a semicolon. The semicolon can *always* be replaced by a period and a new sentence.
    EXAMPLE "Giant Squid may hunt whales. It is hard to be certain."

Each are two independent sentences, so a semicolon is appropriate.

▷ **READING**

Read the passages "The Legendary Kraken," "Underwater Mystery," and "When Squids Attack," and answer the questions that follow.

THE LEGENDARY KRAKEN

The mystery of the Kraken sent shivers down the spines of eighteenth-century sailors. According to legend, the enormous Kraken's sucker tentacles would attach themselves to sailor's ships and pull them down into the dark depths of the sea. There the sailors would drown, or worse yet, be eaten by the monster.

Stories about the Kraken circulated as early as the twelfth century in Norway. In 1753, the Bishop of Bergen wrote that the sea monster Kraken was a "floating island one and a half miles long" that was "full of arms" and could "crush a man-of-war." In his 1871 novel, *20,000 Leagues Under the Sea*, Jules Verne describes "a horrible monster worthy to figure in the legends of the marvelous" that was "a being eight yards long." Although the size of the creature diminished from the eighteenth to the nineteenth century, the horror of it did not.

The giant squid, or *Architeuthis* (pronounced ark-e-TOOTH-iss), is almost certainly the source of the Kraken mystery. Measuring up to seventy feet (as long as two school buses), the giant squid is the largest cephalopod, or marine mollusk, in the world. Weighing anywhere from one to two tons, the Architeuthis has eyes the size of dinner plates and four-inch suckers with a hard, jagged edge in two rows along eight tentacles. Two longer additional tentacles catch food and bring it to the squid's delicate beak. Shaped like a torpedo, the giant squid moves through the ocean by propelling itself using a jet of water forced out of its body by a siphon. It is a carnivore that lives in total darkness in the black depths of the ocean. In fact, the giant squid's natural habitat is so deep and dark that humankind has not yet been able to explore it.

UNDERWATER MYSTERY

"The single most fascinating thing about the giant squid," says marine artist and natural history writer Richard Ellis, "is that it's never been seen by anybody." With a habitat that encompasses most of the world's deep oceans, the giant squid lives 1,000 to 4,000 feet under the surface of the sea. Although bodies of the giant creature have been known to wash up on beaches in Newfoundland, New Zealand, Japan, South

Africa, Norway, Iceland, and Denmark, no living human has seen a healthy, living giant squid in its natural habitat deep in the ocean.

Many attempts were made at the end of the twentieth century to view the mysterious invertebrate in its natural habitat. Using a submersible (a clear, plexiglass sphere that can hold up to four people), scientists lower themselves to depths of 3,000 feet in order to catch a glimpse of the creature. None of the three major expeditions into "inner-space" in the late 1990s yielded sightings of the giant squid. Scientists, however, are not daunted by this and are busy planning their next excursion.

Submersibles are not the only tool scientists use to try and capture images of giant squid. Another approach uses a camera attached to the backs of sperm whales. Sperm whales eat giant squid and scientists hope to capture an image of a living squid when the whales dive to hunt. Robotic submersibles have also been utilized in the effort to view the elusive creature, but to no avail.

WHEN SQUIDS ATTACK

It may be that sailors had good reason to fear the Kraken. In the 1930s the *Brunswick*, a 15,000-ton auxiliary tanker owned by the Royal Norwegian Navy, was attacked three times by a giant squid. Each time the squid would pull up along side the ship, pace it, and run into it, wrapping its tentacles around the ship's hull. Ultimately, the squid lost the battle when, unable to grip the steel with its tentacles, it slid down into the ship's propellers.

Giant squid have been known to attack whales, too. In 1965, a Soviet whaler witnessed a battle between a forty-ton sperm whale and a squid. The strangled whale was later found floating in the sea with the squid's tentacles wrapped around it.

Some experts argue that the giant squid attacks a ship or a whale because it thinks it is food. Others maintain that the squid is trying to catch a ride home. Giant squids live in cold water deep in the sea. This cold water can get trapped above a layer of warm water, pushing the squid to the surface. This may explain why most giant squid sightings have been in areas where cold and warm water currents converge. The squid's natural buoyancy makes it difficult for it to sink beneath the warm water back to the cold where it can live. Some scientists suggest that when a squid attaches itself to a whale, it is merely trying to hitch a ride with a creature it knows dives to great depths. Boats may look like whales to giant squids, which may explain the *Brunswick* attack.

_____ **1.** Which word could be substituted for the word <u>daunted</u> in the second paragraph of the second article without changing the meaning of the sentence?

A angered

B depressed

C excited

D discouraged

_____ **2.** Some experts feel that giant squids attack boats because—

A they are nearsighted

B they think the boats are whales

C they are protecting territory

D they hunt and eat humans

_____ **3.** Which sentence *best* summarizes "An Underwater Mystery"?

A Although many attempts have been made to view the giant squid in its natural habitat, none have been successful so far.

B Scientists are fascinated with the giant squid primarily because they are rare.

C Submersibles and cameras are the best ways to view giant squids in the ocean.

D Denmark, Newfoundland, New Zealand, Japan, and South Africa are the places where giant squid are most likely to be found.

_____ **4.** When warm water currents in the ocean combine with cold water currents—

A the water will be too warm for the giant squid to survive

B a cold water layer may get trapped above a warm water layer

C giant squid will go searching for food

D giant squid will benefit from the warmer temperature

_____ **5.** Which one of the following BEST describes he tone and effect of the first paragraph of the first article?

A Sensational. It describes a frightening sea monster myth.

B Humorous. It grabs the reader's attention by making them laugh at sea monsters.

C Somber. It warns of the dangers of the sea.

D Annoyed. It point out irritating qualities of sea monsters.

_____ **6.** The purpose of these articles is—

A to explain why giant squid are dangerous to whales

B to entertain and to give information about giant squids

C to entertain and to persuade people to support giant squid research

D to frighten and to explain to people why giant squid are dangerous

7. You have decided to search for the giant squid. What sort of preparations do you need to make? Support your response with details and information from the articles.

_____

_____

_____

_____

_____

_____

8. Do you think that all three passages were written by the same person? What evidence do you find to support your view?

_____

_____

_____

_____

_____

_____

COMPOSITION

What other creatures take on an important role in our folklore? Write an informative essay for your classmates about a creature, such as a dragon, the Loch Ness monster, Bigfoot, or a person like Paul Bunyan, which may have existed or does exist. Tell about the folklore behind the "being" and whether or not it is possible to prove the existence of this being. Also, think about the following questions: Do you think it is based on a real being? Why do you think the myth of the creature or person began? What purpose, if any, do you think this "being" and its folktale serves?

Use the following chart to help you organize your thoughts.

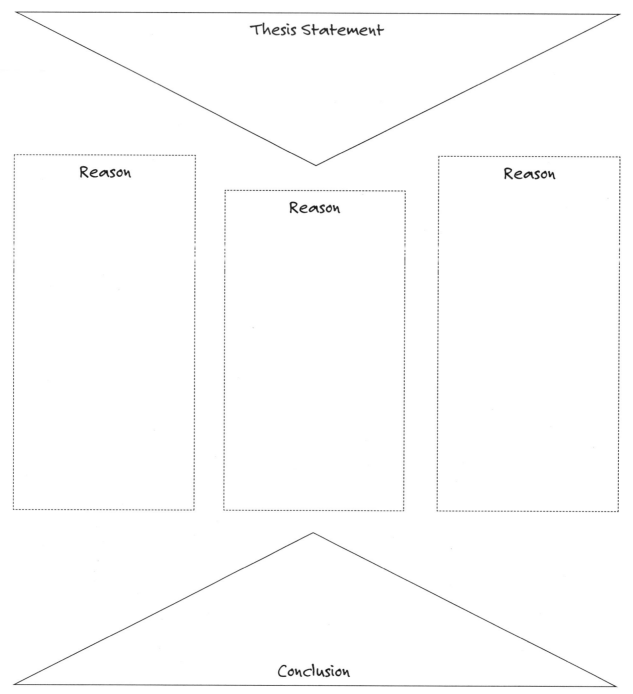

Thesis Statement

Reason

Reason

Reason

Conclusion

EDITING

Read the following passage and determine which word or group of words belongs in each space. Write the letter of the correct answer.

The ship sailed silently in the night. A cool breeze _____ the clouds, revealing
(1)

the full moon hanging in the dark sky. The night was still and calm, the ocean itself

seeming to sleep.

Suddenly, the shipped _____ unsteadily. The motion roused the night
(2)

watchman from his slumber. Rubbing _____ eyes in disbelief, he watched as a
(3)

giant tentacle wrapped itself around the ship's bow. "Captain!" he yelled, although

the word barely _____ out of his throat. "Captain! The Kraken!"
(4)

The night air burst with the shouts of the captain and his crew as they readied

themselves for the biggest battle of their lives.

____ **1. A** stirred
    B did stirred
    C stirring
    D had stir

____ **2. A** did rocked
    B rocked
    C rocking
    D has rocked

____ **3. A** her
    B his
    C their
    D the

____ **4. A** has croaked
    B croak
    C croaks
    D croaked

DISCUSSION QUESTIONS

The focus of this unit is a personal narrative involving discovery. To encourage discussion of the topic, ask the following questions:

- Have you ever had an experience that did not meet your expectations? What happened? What was that like?

- Have you ever surprised yourself by enjoying something you thought you would hate? If so, what?

- Do you think people should be made to do things they don't consider fun? Why or why not?

READING—*Inferring*

As students read the passage, ask them to consider the following questions:

- What does the narrator expect to happen in the first paragraph? How do these expectations affect her response?

- What kind of relationship does the narrator have with her siblings?

- Why won't the narrator tell her parents it was a good vacation?

COMPOSITION—*Organizing Ideas*

Ask students to pick an event in their lives where they discovered something new about themselves. Then have them write answers to the following questions:

- What is _____ similar to? In what ways?

- What is _____ different from? In what ways?

- Are there any songs or poems about _____ ?

- Is there anything I remember from books, television, or movies about _____ ?

EDITING—Whoever *and* Whomever

Remind students about these rules regarding the use of *whoever* and *whomever*.

- Use the *-ever* suffix when *who* or *whom* can fit into two clauses in the sentence.

    EXAMPLE Send it to whoever/whomever requires it. Send it to *him*. *He* requires it.

    Because *him* and *he* can be substituted into both clauses, the *-ever* suffix should be used.

- To determine whether to use *whoever* or *whomever*, use the following rule:

    him + he = whoever

    him + him = whomever

    Therefore, *Send it to <u>whoever</u> requires it.*

YOU CALL THIS A VACATION?

When I was thirteen years old, my parents rented a home in the Sierra Nevada Mountains and took my whole family away for two weeks in the summer. It was supposed to be a great treat, but when we got to the "house" my siblings and I discovered that it was just a cabin, and not even a nice cabin at that. All the other homes in the area were beautiful and big, but ours was a dumpy old wreck that looked like it was about to fall down.

To make matters worse, the dumpy wreck didn't have a television. It didn't even have a radio. What were my brother and sister and I to do for two whole weeks without any access to the outside world? We were desperate. We complained. We begged our parents to take us back to the comforts of suburbia. Nothing doing. We were stuck. To add insult to injury, my parents proceeded to enjoy themselves, regardless of how miserable we, their offspring, became.

The first few days were an agony of boredom. We lay listlessly about the cabin, counting our mosquito bites for entertainment. I had twenty-five, a record. My sister had seventeen. My brother became obsessed with bug repellent, slathering it on in order to avoid being bitten. It was going to be the longest two weeks in my life.

After about three days, however, a transformation began to occur. My siblings and I began to talk to each other. With nothing better to do, we played games and told stories for entertainment. One night when our parents were out, we wrote a play, using pillows and chairs as characters. When our parents returned, the main room of the cabin was transformed into a theater, with every piece of furniture a character in our play. We began to challenge each other creatively, trying to outdo each other with fun things to do.

The biggest revelation on that trip for me, however, was that I unearthed a love of reading. With no TV to distract me, reading became an escape into different worlds. Suddenly, an entire realm of imagination opened up before me, as diverse and entertaining as the different books I read. I was no longer bored-out-of-my-skull, but rather caught up in the new horizons my books revealed.

Another lifetime enjoyment that emerged from that trip was a love of nature. Previous to this trip to the Sierra Nevada region, my siblings and I had not spent that much time in the wilderness. Now, with nothing but time on our hands, we discovered how rewarding and fascinating a walk in the woods can be. The mountains loomed around us, filled with evergreens. They were so high they still had snowy peaks, even in the middle of summer. One day my sister

UNIT 4

and I took a hike by ourselves. We came upon a meadow and lay back amongst the grass and wildflowers, watching the clouds drift lazily overhead. A whole afternoon passed and we didn't even notice it, so content were we to watch the clouds roll through the sky.

Although we would never have admitted it to our parents, that trip was one of the best that my siblings and I ever had. We learned to enjoy each others company and work together. Instead of bickering and arguing as we were used to doing, we had fun. We also learned how to engage our minds and our creativity in every day tasks. I've never asked my parents, but I wonder if that was what they had in mind the all along . . . ?

____ **1.** Which word could be substituted for the word revelation in the fifth paragraph without changing the meaning of the sentence?

A horror

B enjoyment

C discovery

D reward

____ **2.** Which one of the following did the siblings NOT do on their trip?

A create a play using furniture as characters

B compare mosquito bites

C learn how to climb rocks

D play games together

____ **3.** What is the main idea of the second paragraph?

A The cabin was run down and did not live up to expectations.

B My parents commiserated with us.

C Learning to amuse oneself is a valuable skill.

D Bug repellent helps prevent mosquito bites.

____ **4.** Based on the passage, this vacation may be BEST described as—

A horrible

B rugged

C surprising

D decadent

____ **5.** The tone of this passage can BEST be described as—

A lighthearted

B angry

C joyous

D bitter

____ **6.** Which one of the following is a fact stated in the passage?

A Our parents proceeded to enjoy themselves.

B The first few days were an agony of boredom.

C The peaks of the mountains

D We were desperate.

7. After reading the passage, do you think the author would encourage other people to take their children on such a vacation? Explain your answer using what you know from the passage and what you know from your own experience.

_____

_____

_____

_____

_____

_____

_____

COMPOSITION

What discoveries have you made from a difficult experience? How did you make them? Did anyone help you? Write an amusing essay for your local newspaper describing your experience. Choose one aspect of it to describe in detail. Tell what the experience was, why it was difficult, how you faced it, and how you feel about it now. Use the word web below to help you organize your thoughts. Be sure to express the transformation you made by the experience.

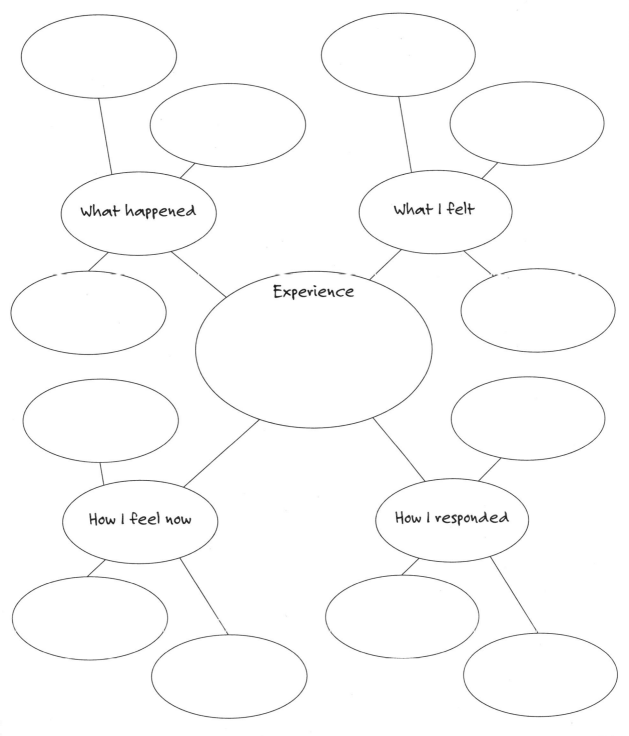

▶ EDITING

Read the following passage and determine which type or error, if any, appears in the underlined sections. Write the letter of the correct answer.

Dear Sarah,

Last week was the eeriest week I've spent in my whole life. At first, Debbie and I had nothing to do, <u>so we had a misquito bite contest.</u> I won because I had
(1)
twenty-five bites. But then, on the third day, we found a book of ghost stories written by my grandfather. Every night, we scared each other by reading a new story. <u>By the end of the week believe it or not we were writing</u> our own ghost
(2)
stories. <u>We folded them into the book maybe one day</u> our grandchildren will scare
(3)
each other with them. <u>What a weak in the woods!</u>
(4)

Ghostly yours,

Jennlee

____ **1. A** Spelling error
     B Capitalization error
     C Punctuation error
     D No error

____ **2. A** Spelling error
     B Capitalization error
     C Punctuation error
     D No error

____ **3. A** Spelling error
     B Capitalization error
     C Punctuation error
     D No error

____ **4. A** Spelling error
     B Capitalization error
     C Punctuation error
     D No error

UNIT 5

DISCUSSION QUESTIONS

The focus of this unit is Ernest Shackleton's 1914 *Endurance* expedition to the Antarctic. To encourage discussion, ask the following questions:

- What do you think it was like to travel to the extremes of the Antarctic in 1914? How would it be different today?
- In the Antarctic, most of the food people eat goes directly to generating heat. Even when a person feels comfortably warm, they are using over half their total caloric intake just to maintain their body temperature. Given this knowledge, what measures do you suppose Shackleton and his crew took in order to keep warm?
- Have you ever wanted to travel to unexplored territories? Why or why not?

READING—*Identifying Supporting Ideas*

As students read the first passage, ask them to do the following:

- List the main idea in each paragraph.
- Have them list all the sentences which support the main idea
- Have them change the order of the events in the passage. Ask them if this changes their understanding of the passage.

COMPOSITION—*Developing Ideas*

Discuss with students the difference between "official" explorers like Christopher Columbus, those sanctioned by the government, and individuals who pursue adventure on their own.

- What drives governments or institutions to support these expeditions?
- What drives individuals to embark on dangerous expeditions?

EDITING—*Identifying Prepositions*

Remind students of these guidelines when using prepositions.

- To determine if a word is a preposition, see if it makes sense in the following sentence. If it does, it's a preposition.
  The dog ran _____ the hoop.
- Use *on* with expressions that indicate the time of an occurrence.
  EXAMPLE Shackleton's expedition left on August 8, 1914.
- *Of* should never be used in place of *have*.
  CORRECT Shackleton should have set camp earlier.
  INCORRECT Shackleton should of set camp earlier.
- *Between* refers to two. *Among* is used for three or more.
  EXAMPLES Divide the supplies between the two of you.
                        Divide the supplies among the three of you.
- *Into* implies entrance, whereas *in* does not.
  EXAMPLES Shackleton crawled into the boat.
                        Shackleton was waiting in the boat.

READING

Read the passage "Fortitudine Vincimus—By Endurance We Conquer," and answer the questions that follow.

FORTITUDINE VINCIMUS—
BY ENDURANCE WE CONQUER

Ernest Shackleton had little understanding of how true his family's motto *Fortitudine Vincimus* (by endurance we conquer) would prove to be when he set out on his famous expedition in August of 1914. Mere days after war had broken out in Europe, Shackleton and his crew set sail for the Antarctic on the ship he had named *Endurance*. Their quest: to be the first men to cross the Antarctic continent on foot.

When it was just one day's sail from the Antarctic continent, however, the *Endurance* became trapped in pack ice and remained there for ten months. Shackleton hoped to be able to camp on the ship through the Antarctic winter, but it soon became clear that the ship, no matter how sturdy, could not bear the pressure of the mighty ice packs. Realizing the *Endurance* was about to be crushed, the men abandoned ship and camped on drifting ice floes for the next five months. When the ice disintegrated, Shackleton and his men set sail in the three lifeboats they had managed to cart off the *Endurance* and tow by foot over the ice. On April 12th, 1916, after treacherous sailing on the Weddell Sea in open boats, Shackleton and his crew landed on Elephant Island—their first steps on land in sixteen months.

Not Safe Yet

While landing on Elephant Island was a great triumph, it didn't get Shackleton and his crew out of their predicament. The nearest food and shelter was 800 stormy miles northwest of them on South Georgia Island. Leaving twenty-two of his men behind with only two lifeboats and some old tents for shelter, Shackleton and five other men set sail.

The long months of hardship took their toll on Shackleton and his men. In the rough sea, surrounded by huge bergs of ice, Frank Worsley, the ship's captain, wrote, "Swans of weird shape pecked at our planks, a gondola steered by a giraffe ran foul of us, which much amused a duck sitting on a crocodile's head. Just then a bear, leaning over the top of a mosque, nearly clawed our sail . . . All the strange, fantastic shapes rose and fell in stately cadence with a rustling, whispering sound and hollow echoes to the thudding seas. . . ." The men and their gear were soaked, and ice kept forming on the ship, making it so heavy that they were forced to continuously chip away at it as it formed in order to stay afloat.

Shackleton and his men experienced one narrow escape after another. On the eleventh day of their journey, after several days of inclement weather, Shackleton wrote:

> "I called to the other men that the sky was clearing, and then a moment later I realized that what I had seen was not a rift in the clouds but the white crest of an enormous wave. During twenty-six years' experience of the ocean in all its moods I had not encountered a wave so gigantic. It was a mighty upheaval of the ocean, a thing quite apart from the big white-capped seas that had been our tireless enemies for many days. I shouted 'For God's sake, hold on! It's got us.' Then came a moment of suspense that seemed drawn out into hours. White surged the foam of the breaking sea around us. We felt our boat lifted and flung forward like a cork in breaking surf. We were in a seething chaos of tortured water; but somehow the boat lived through it, half full of water, sagging to the dead weight and shuddering under the blow. We baled with the energy of men fighting for life, flinging the water over the sides with every receptacle that came to our hands."

Sixteen days after they had left Elephant Island, Shackleton and his crew landed safely on South Georgia.

The Impossible Crossing

Once again, however, Shackleton's journey was not finished. Although he and his men had reached South Georgia, they were seventeen mountainous miles from the whaling station that they were trying to reach. No one had ever traversed the icy mountain range of South Georgia simply because it was thought to be impassable. Yet Shackleton and his men had to succeed in crossing the range to survive.

Walking continuously for twenty-four hours, Shackleton and two of his crew ascended glaciers, slid down slopes, crossed shallow lakes, and descended through waterfalls in order to reach the Stromness whaling station. They arrived exhausted but triumphant, with matted hair and clothes that hadn't been washed in nearly a year. Encountering two small boys, Shackleton asked them where he could find the manager's house. The boys turned and ran away in fright.

On August 30, 1917, after four unsuccessful attempts to land on Elephant Island, Shackleton returned to rescue his remaining crew. Miraculously, every man survived the harrowing journey of the *Endurance*.

____ **1.** Which word could be substituted for the word <u>traversed</u> in the first paragraph of the last article without changing the meaning of the sentence?

A carried

B explored

C examined

D crossed

____ **2.** Which one of the following did Shackleton and his crew NOT experience on their expedition?

A massive waves

B icy winds

C tornadoes

D exhaustion

____ **3.** Which sentence BEST reflects the main idea of the second paragraph of the first article?

A The *Endurance* became trapped in pack ice and had to be abandoned.

B Shackleton bravely led his men to safety.

C Giant waves battered Shackleton and his crew.

D Shackleton's crew despaired when the *Endurance* was crushed by ice.

____ **4.** Based on the passages, Shackleton's expedition can best be described as—

A a heroic conquering of impossible circumstances

B a humorous misadventure

C a frightening lesson in mortality

D an amazing documentation of sea life

____ **5.** The tone of these passages can be described as—

A humorous

B wry

C dry

D suspenseful

____ **6.** Which one of the following is an opinion stated in the last passage?

A Shackleton and his men were extremely brave to succeed in crossing the range to survive.

B Shackleton crossed a mountain range that most considered impassible.

C Shackleton and his crew descended through waterfalls to reach the whaling station.

D Shackleton landed seventeen miles from the whaling station.

7. After reading the passage, do you think Shackleton felt proud at the end of his adventure? Explain your answer using what you know from the passage and what you know from your own experience.

_____

_____

_____

_____

_____

_____

_____

8. Though each passage is a continuation of Shackleton and his crew's experience, how is each passage different in its narrative presentation?

_____

_____

_____

_____

_____

_____

_____

_____

UNIT 5

COMPOSITION

Shackleton wrote of his *Endurance* expedition, "We had suffered, starved and triumphed, groveled down yet grasped at glory, grown bigger in the bigness of the whole. We had seen God in His splendours, heard the text that Nature renders. We had reached the naked soul of man."

Is it necessary to risk death in order to "grasp at glory"? Why do you think humans have been fascinated with exploring new territories through the ages? Are there any new territories left to explore? Write an essay for your classmates discussing your response to one of these questions. Tell what your thoughts are and support them with detailed reasons.

Use the chart below to help you organize your thoughts.

UNIT 5

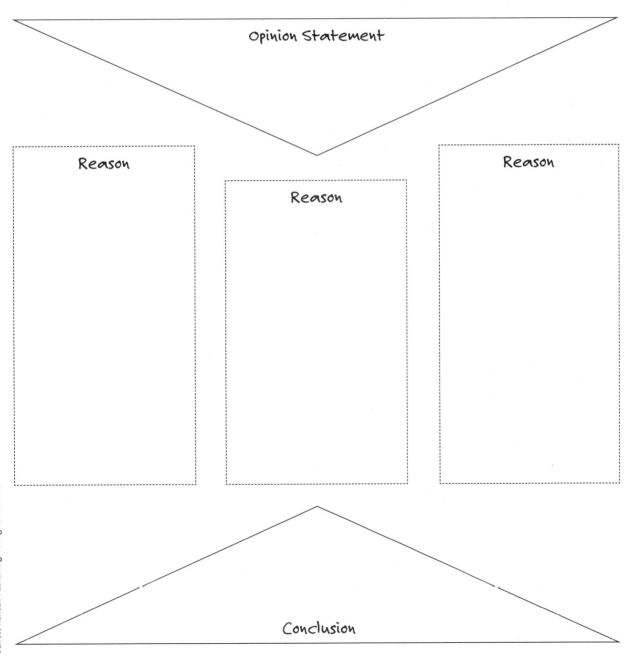

Opinion Statement

Reason

Reason

Reason

Conclusion

EDITING

Read the following passage and determine which type of error, if any, appears in the underlined sections. Write the letter of the correct answer.

<u>another problem Shackleton and his crew faced while camping on the ice was</u>
(1)
killer whales. <u>Spotting a seal, the wails would dive deep down under the sea</u> and
(2)
then smash up through the ice, seizing the seal in its mouth. Shackleton and his

men found a <u>whole twenty-five feet wide</u> that had been created by a killer whale.
(3)
The expedition photographer, Frank Hurley, <u>hearing the whales beneath him as he</u>
(4)
<u>crossed the ice with his team of dogs described what he felt;</u>

> The whales behind...broke through the thin ice as though it were
> tissue paper, and, I fancy, were so staggered by the strange sight that
> met their eyes, that for a moment they hesitated. Never in my life
> have I looked upon more loathsome creatures.

____ **1. A** Spelling Error
    B Capitalization error
    C Punctuation error
    D No error

____ **2. A** Spelling error
    B Capitalization error
    C Punctuation error
    D No error

____ **3. A** Spelling error
    B Capitalization error
    C Punctuation error
    D No error

____ **4. A** Spelling error
    B Capitalization error
    C Punctuation error
    D No error

DISCUSSION QUESTIONS

The focus of this unit is opinions about high sports salaries. To encourage discussion of the topic, ask the following questions:

- What are some of the reasons why sports salaries are so high? (Think about TV and advertising revenues.)
- What affect (if any) do you think high salaries have on the players?
- Do you think high salaries make sports stars good role models? Why or why not?

READING—*Recognizing Points of View*

As students read the passages, ask them to think about the following questions:

- Is the primary intent of the author of the passages to inform, to persuade, to express, or to entertain?
- What clues are there in the article which show the author's intent?
- How does the author's perspective affect the style of the text?

COMPOSITION—*Using Imagination to Spark Ideas*

Ask students to imagine they are the bank account of a highly paid sports star.

- Have students brainstorm a list of opinions the bank account may have about itself. (For example, how good it feels to be big, how they like having part of them spent on charity, and so on.)
- Have students debate in small groups about the pros and cons of high salaries for sports stars.

EDITING—Affect *and* Effect

Remind students about the following:

- *Affect* is most commonly used to mean "to influence."
  EXAMPLE Winning the game affected my mood.
- *Effect* means "to bring about or execute."
  EXAMPLE What effect did her final shot have?
- The sentence *Winning the game may effect revenues* implies that winning will cause revenues to occur, whereas *Winning the game may affect revenues* implies that winning may have an impact on revenues that have already occurred.

▷ **READING**

Read the passages "Sports Heroes Deserve High Salaries" and "What's Up With Sports Salaries?", and answer the questions that follow.

SPORTS HEROES DESERVE HIGH SALARIES

Some people argue that today's top athletes are overpaid. I couldn't disagree with them more.

Sports heroes are paid just what we consumers think they deserve. Americans keep spending more and more dollars in order to watch the sports they love. If team owners are going to make hundreds of millions of dollars off of their teams, why shouldn't the players profit? In today's stock-option economy, it makes sense that players should reap a greater percentage of what they sow. If sports stars made $38,000 like the average middle-class American family, it would mean that all those sports profits would go directly to already wealthy team owners. Why should the owners get all the dough?

Owners argue that outrageous salaries are forcing them to raise ticket prices, but that's just because they don't want to cut into their own profits. They could easily take home a few less million a year, but they won't. And you know what? Ticket prices aren't based on players' salaries. They're based on good old capitalist supply and demand. If fans are willing to pay $86 to watch a basketball game, why should owners charge less? Sports are for profit, for goodness sake, not for fun.

The way it works now, players' salaries reflect the temperate waters in the revenue pool. As long as Americans are willing to shell out big bucks for their favorite teams, athletes deserve their portion of the pie. Team owners are making more money than ever. In 1986, the Cleveland Indians franchise was purchased for $45 million. Thirteen years later, the franchise was sold for $320 million—over seven times its 1986 buying price. That same year, pro football's Washington Redskins franchise was purchased for a record $800 million.

Team owners know that they will make money on an $800 million investment. If they are making hundreds of millions, why shouldn't team players make millions themselves? After all, it's their effort and skill that brings in the crowds. Isn't it only fair they should receive a fair share of the profits?

HIGHEST SALARIES IN PROFESSIONAL SPORTS*				
	Basketball	Baseball	Football	Hockey
1988	$3 million	$2.34 million	$1.96 million	$900,000
1999	$17.4 million	$11 million	$5.87 million	$10.36 million

*Does not include signing bonuses or incentives

WHAT'S UP WITH
SPORTS SALARIES?

Many things don't make sense in this crazy world. But in my opinion, one of the biggest mysteries facing us in the 21st century has got to be professional sport salaries. What is going on with them? According to statistics, from 1950 to 1998, the average American worker's salary rose 13 times the 1950 rate—from roughly $2,800 to $38,800. The average professional baseball player's salary, however, rose a whopping 100 times the 1950 rate—from approximately $13,000 in 1950 to $1.4 million in 1998. That's a pretty big difference.

What I want to know is where does it all end? Is anyone besides me concerned that Michael Jordan made $33 million dollars during his final season with the Chicago Bulls? What does this impossibly high salary signify in a world where children go hungry and schools languish for lack of funds?

This is not to lay the burden of world hunger at Mr. Jordan's size thirteen feet. But what do these high salaries reveal about our values as a culture?

More and more, the sports pages of the newspaper are starting to look like the financial pages. An NBA child cracker-jack signs a six-year, $126 million contract. A rookie receives a record $15 million. One player's $10 million salary is higher than another team's entire payroll.

It's not that I object to people making money. It's just that I wonder about skills such as throwing a ball through a hoop or kicking a ball through two poles being more highly valued than, say, running the Free World. The president of the United States makes $250,000 a year. A high school teacher averages $35,000.

Then there's the fact that woman sports stars still earn less than their male counterparts.

All this is not to denigrate the skill and talent of professional athletes. Or even to argue that they don't deserve to be well paid for their efforts. I just wonder what these astronomical salaries mean in terms of regular people. It used to be that young kids knew the team number of their favorite player. Now they know the number in his bank account.

1. Which word could be substituted for languish in the fourth

paragraph of the last article without changing the meaning of the sentence?

A thrive

B desire

C decline

D deplete

2. The author of the first article feels that sports stars—

A are paid too much because their high salaries necessitate high ticket prices

B should be paid a lot of money because the owners are making a lot of money

C are childish and should be better role models

D should be paid high salaries because sports are hard on athletes' bodies

UNIT 6

_____ **3.** According to the table, which sport saw the highest increase in salary from 1988 to 1999?

A hockey

B football

C baseball

D basketball

_____ **4.** According to the second article—

A high sport salaries reflect American values

B high sport salaries reflect high revenues

C players earn their high salaries when they win games

D the President of the United States should play basketball

_____ **5.** The tone of the first article can best be described as—

A informal

B formal

C somber

D analytical

_____ **6.** The purpose of these articles is to—

A to express outrage at the high cost of sports tickets

B to express an opinion about high sport salaries

C to persuade people to boycott expensive sports

D to educate people about high sport salaries

7. Explain your opinion on the topic of professional sports salaries. Use details from the articles, along with your own experience to support your opinion.

_____

_____

_____

_____

_____

_____

_____

_____

_____

_____

8. In your own words, compare the arguments in the two articles. How are they similar? How are they different?

_____

_____

_____

_____

_____

_____

_____

_____

_____

_____

UNIT 6

COMPOSITION

Imagine that you own a professional sports team in a city that does not have a big television market and hence does not bring in large television revenues for broadcasting games. You want to assemble the best team possible but you don't have the same money to offer for salaries as teams in larger cities such as Los Angeles or New York. What do you think about your situation? What are your options? Is it fair? Write an editorial for your city's paper explaining your perspective.

Use the following chart to help you organize your ideas.

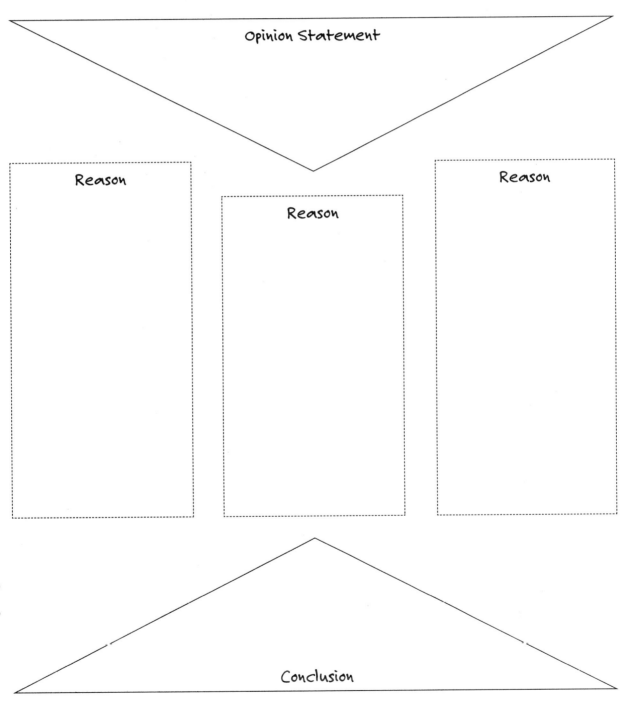

UNIT 6

▷ EDITING

Read the following passage and determine which word or group of words belongs in each space. Write the letter of the correct answer.

···

My brother and I went to the _____ basketball game I've seen in a long time.
(1)

It starred our father and a group of his friends. They are teachers and they were

playing against the administrators of the school where they teach. The game was a

benefit to raise money for the sports program at our school. The _____ thing about
(2)

it was that it was played with donkeys. The court was covered with a protective

surface and then all the players came out seated atop their animal partners. Being

seated atop a donkey sure _____ my father's game! I think donkeys are even
(3)

_____ than my brother and me.
(4)

____ **1. A** most excitingest
      B most exciting
      C mostest exciting
      D most excitinger

____ **2. A** incredible
      B incrediblest
      C most incrediblest
      D mostest incredible

____ **3. A** did effected
      B did affected
      C effected
      D affected

____ **4. A** most stubbornest
      B more stubbornest
      C most stubborn
      D more stubborn

UNIT 6

DISCUSSION QUESTIONS

The focus of this unit is a personal narrative. To encourage discussion of the topic, ask the following questions:

- Have you ever imagined what an experience will be like before it happens?
- How is what you imagined different than the reality? How is it similar?
- Is there some place that you would love to visit? Why? What do you think it will be like?

READING—*Summarizing*

As students read the passage, ask them to do the following:

- List the events in the passage.
- Summarize the passage in a short paragraph using their list.
- Think of an event from their own lives and have them list the action of the event and summarize it.

COMPOSITION—*Generating Ideas*

Ask students to brainstorm a list of places they have always wanted to visit. Then have students break off into groups to compare and discuss their choices.

- Students with simialr places can compare and contrast their reasons for wanting to visit the place.
- Students with different choices can explain to others the wonders of the place.

EDITING—*Avoiding Misplaced or Dangling Modifiers*

Remind students that a *modifier* is a word, phrase, or clause that limits or qualifies the sense of another word or word group. Have students review the following guidelines:

- If you start a sentence with an action, place the actor immediately after.
  UNCLEAR While crossing the street, the taxi nearly swiped her.
  CLEAR While crossing the street, she was nearly swiped by a taxi.
  OR
  She was nearly swiped by a taxi while crossing the street.
- Place modifiers near the words they modify.
  UNCLEAR I have some bagels he gave me in my lunch bag.
  CLEAR In my lunch bag, I have some bagels he gave me.

UNIT 7

▶ READING

Read the passage "New York, New York," and answer the questions that follow.

NEW YORK, NEW YORK

When I was sixteen, I got to go to on a trip to New York City with my best friend. I was so excited! As a small girl, I had played a game called "Apartment Girls in New York City" and now I was actually going to go see the famous city on my own. I imagined bright lights, Broadway shows, sophisticated people, and marvelous museums.

Getting to New York was no small feat. My parents, although raised in a large city themselves, had a great distrust of the Big Apple and did not want me to go there. My older sister had been allowed to take a trip to New York when she was seventeen, but that had been a school trip, organized and chaperoned by a teacher. By the time I got to high school, that school trip was no longer available. I was devastated, but my mother was thrilled. She didn't want me, her baby, to go all the way across the country.

My parents, however, wanted to appear fair. They couldn't tell me straight-out that they didn't want me to go, because I would argue that my sister had been allowed to go and, by the same token, I should be allowed, too. No, my parents were cagey. They said if I could earn the money for my airfare from San Diego to New York, they would permit me to go. Now, my parents knew that I didn't have any money in the bank. They knew that I didn't have a job. They also knew that didn't have a lot of time to earn enough money to pay for my ticket by working after school and on weekends. But I outsmarted them. I got a job. I worked whenever I wasn't in school for three months until I had the money to pay for my flight. Boy, were my parents surprised.

It's not that my parents were ogres, they were just worried about their youngest child leaving the nest. The night before we left, my girlfriend and I were ablaze with excitement. We couldn't sleep and spent the whole night discussing what we wanted to do and where we wanted to go in "The City". On the plane, I was a bundle of nerves and excitement. New York! The Big Apple! I couldn't wait.

When we arrived, we first headed to New Jersey, where my friend's family had relatives. There was snow on the ground—a novelty to someone raised in San Diego. I had New York pizza for the first time in New Jersey. It was delicious! After our brief visit, we drove through the Lincoln Tunnel to the great metropolis itself. My heart was pounding. My friend and I were buzzing with an excitement that was electric. We were here at last. We. Were. Here.

We got out of the car and entered the hotel where we would be staying. My friend's father was taking us all to dinner and a Broadway show; we had to prepare ourselves. We dressed in our nicest dresses and put on our winter coats. December in New York is quite different from December in San Diego. We bundled up and stepped outside. The lights twinkled, pedestrians zipped past us on their way to important things, and an icy wind blew down the street, chilling my friend and me to the bone, all the way through our heavy winter coats.

We looked at each other.

"It's cold," she said. "I hate it. I want to go home."

And we laughed.

1. Which word could be substituted for the word <u>cagey</u> in the third paragraph without changing the meaning of the sentence?
   A funnier
   B angrier
   C craftier
   D sillier

2. Which one of the following did the author NOT do on her trip?
   A eat New York pizza in New Jersey
   B get prepared to go out for dinner and a show
   C ride the subway
   D buzz with excitement

3. What is the main idea of the second paragraph?
   A My parents did not want me to go to New York.
   B My parents liked my sister better than me.
   C My parents encouraged me to travel and be adventurous.
   D My parents supported the idea of a trip.

4. Based on the passage, the author's parents can be BEST described as—
   A cruel but sympathetic
   B controlling and unfair
   C protective but fair
   D free-spirited and liberal

5. The tone of this passage can *best* be described as—
   A light
   B dark
   C somber
   D hysterical

6. Which one of the following is an opinion stated in the passage?
   A December in New York is quite different from December in San Diego.
   B I had New York pizza for the first time in New Jersey.
   C My friend's father was taking us all to dinner and a Broadway show.
   D We headed to New Jersey where my friend's family had relatives.

7. After reading the passage, why do you think the friends laughed? Explain your answer using what you know from the passage and what you know from your own experience.

_____

_____

_____

_____

_____

_____

_____

_____

_____

COMPOSITION

Is there a city or country that you have always wanted to visit? Write an essay for your classmates describing the place, telling them why you want to go, and persuading them to visit the place with you. Use vivid details, and be sure to organize the details in logical order.

Use the word web below to help you organize your thoughts.

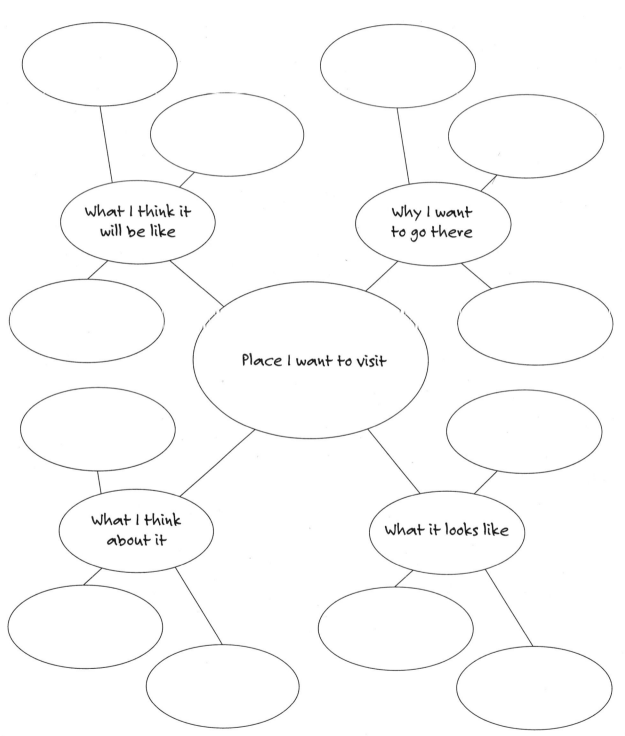

EDITING

Read the following passage and determine which type of error, if any, appears in the underlined sections. Write the letter of the correct answer.

One of my favorite museums in New York City <u>is the Cloisters Museum.</u>
(1)

<u>located near the northwestern tip of Manhattan,</u> the museum is filled with art from

the Middle Ages. It is built like an old cloister and parts of the buildings are actually

from medieval structures. <u>Inside are many objects; like reliquaries and tapestries.</u>
(2)

One of <u>the most gourgeous tapestries shows</u> a unicorn surrounded by flowers. The
(3)

tapestry is so beautiful that it makes me wonder what the people who wove the

tapestry were like. The Cloisters also has <u>an amazing herb garden and a wonderful</u>
(4)

<u>view of the hudson River.</u>

____ **1. A** Spelling error
    B Capitalization error
    C Punctuation error
    D No error

____ **2. A** Spelling error
    B Capitalization error
    C Punctuation error
    D No error

____ **3. A** Spelling error
    B Capitalization error
    C Punctuation error
    D No error

____ **4. A** Spelling error
    B Capitalization error
    C Punctuation error
    D No error

UNIT 7

DISCUSSION QUESTIONS

The focus of this unit is Woody Guthrie and America in the 1930s. To encourage discussion of the topic, ask students:

- What do you know about the Great Depression? What was America like at that time?
- Who are migrant farm workers and what do they do?
- Do you listen to music that has political or social overtones?

READING—*Recognizing the Author's Point of View*

- Ask students if the author supports labor unions.
- What evidence do they find for this?
- Have students list words from the passages that seem "loaded" in favor of the author's point of view.

COMPOSITION—*Prewriting*

Ask students to freewrite about any workers, situations and/or human rights issues in today's world that they know about.

- Working in groups, have students share their ideas and narrow the group's ideas to a theme about workers.
- Then have students write a song about their topic.

EDITING—*Reviewing Double Negatives*

Review rules regarding double negatives:

- Using two negative words to make a thought negative is called a double negative.

    INCORRECT Woody Guthrie didn't write no anti-worker songs.

    Didn't and *no* cancel each other out. Only one negative word is needed to make the thought negative.

    CORRECT   Woody Guthrie didn't write any anti-worker songs.

READING

Read the passages "An American Original," "Woody Guthrie and Labor Unions," and "Guthrie the Humanist," and answer the questions that follow.

AN AMERICAN ORIGINAL

Woody Guthrie was an American original. Born in Okemah, Oklahoma in 1912, he first began tramping and singing about the trials of the working class during the 1930s. No stranger to hard times himself, Woody was influenced deeply by the hardship he saw others experiencing. The Great Depression had America in its grip and an unprecedented twenty-five percent of the population was unemployed. Then, in 1935, severe drought and dust storms plagued Oklahoma, Texas, Arkansas, and much of the Midwest. Banks foreclosed on farmers who were unable to pay their mortgages. Woody took to the road with thousands of other out-of-work farmers, heading for California and the promise of employment.

What he saw on the road had a profound impact on him. Men, women, and children by the hundreds had been completely dispossessed. They had lost their belongings, their dignity, their community, and their livelihood and were trying to build new lives for themselves by leaving what they had always known in search of work. It aroused a sense of indignation and compassion in Guthrie that he never lost.

Once in California, however, the trials of these migrant workers became worse than anything they had experienced on the road. Rather than reaching the "Promised Land" that had been advertised to them in flyers, these workers found only exploitation and humiliation at the hands of wealthy and powerful landowners.

With his trademark mix of wry humor and compassion, Woody wrote a song, "Do Re Mi", that eloquently captured the crux of the migrant workers' problem. Using simple language and rhyming, Guthrie evokes the troubles migrant workers faced when they arrived in California.

Here are some lyrics from the song:

> California is a garden of Eden, a paradise to live in or to see
> But believe it or not, you won't find it so hot
> If you ain't got the do re mi

In an introduction to a collection of Guthrie's songs, John Steinbeck wrote that in Woody Guthrie, "There is the will of the people to endure and fight against oppression. I think we call this the American spirit."

WOODY GUTHRIE AND LABOR UNIONS

The nineteenth-century industrialization of America created vast amounts of wealth for a small number of people, while working people saw few benefits of their labor. They lived in slums, had dangerous working conditions, and could be laid off on a moment's notice. Workers organized unions to protect themselves and their interests. Not surprisingly, owners and the government were hostile to union organizing, often employing violent tactics to break unions and dissuade workers from joining.

In the 1930s, however, the Great Depression and the Dust Bowl resulted in many Americans losing their jobs. Suddenly, the "working class" was not the only group to experience hardship and instability in the American workplace. The average yearly wage fell forty percent in three years, from $2,300 to $1,500. Across the country, Americans clamored for some sort of social security from their government and their employers. President Franklin Delano Roosevelt instigated the New Deal in American politics, aimed at addressing these growing concerns.

Woody Guthrie became an integral part of the American Labor Movement during the 1930s and maintained his connection with labor throughout his life. He went from singing about the plight of the workers to singing about their banding together to do something about it. Guthrie firmly believed in the right of workers to protection, a living wage, and dignity. Of his singing, he stated, "I'm an educator, not an entertainer."

Through his singing at rallies, migrant camps, and railway cars, Woody Guthrie came to epitomize the working class experience in the United States. In a 1943 review of his autobiography, *Bound for Glory*, the *New Yorker* magazine wrote, "Someday people are going to wake up to the fact that Woody Guthrie and the ten thousand songs that leap and tumble off the strings of his music box are a national possession, like Yellowstone and Yosemite, and part of the best stuff this country has to show the world."

GUTHRIE THE HUMANIST

Above all, Woody Guthrie was a humanist who believed in the integrity and value of all human life. In his political work, his art, his writing, and his singing, he critiqued a political system that promoted such discrepancies between rich and poor and put forth the idea that all Americans should share in the wealth of the United States.

For Guthrie, America was too promising, too gorgeous, and too special to belong only to those who owned large parcels of property. He believed that the inequalities that existed in America were merely promises not kept. He considered those promises a challenge that would inspire hope and commitment from those who had been deprived. His was a hopeful view of a world dedicated to the good of all.

UNIT 8

____ 1. Which word could be substituted for dispossessed in the second paragraph of the first article without changing the meaning of the sentence?

   A disorganized

   B deprived

   C disrupted

   D disgusted

____ 2. According to the first article, what happened in 1935?

   A The Midwest was hit by drought and dust storms.

   B President Roosevelt established the New Deal.

   C Woody Guthrie wrote "This Land Was Made for You and Me."

   D Woody Guthrie supported Labor Unions.

____ 3. What is the main idea of the last article?

   A Woody Guthrie was a strong supporter of labor unions.

   B Woody Guthrie left Oklahoma for California.

   C Woody Guthrie was an American original.

   D Woody Guthrie was a humanist.

____ 4. Why did Guthrie support the labor unions?

   A Because he witnessed the hardship of migrant workers first-hand.

   B Because he believed that America was great.

   C Because he was disappointed by the New Deal.

   D Because the average wage fell forty percent in three years.

____ 5. Woody Guthrie considered himself an educator because—

   A he wanted to show the world how to be a folk singer

   B he preferred teaching to singing

   C he wanted to let working people know they had rights through his songs

   D he taught high school for a large portion of his life

____ 6. The author of the last passage probably believes that—

   A Woody Guthrie is the greatest American folk singer

   B "Do Re Mi" is Guthrie's most political song

   C Guthrie showed integrity in questioning American values

   D Guthrie showed weakness by always rambling and never staying in one place

7. Why do you think John Steinbeck described Guthrie as embodying the American spirit? Use examples for the articles

_____

_____

_____

_____

_____

_____

8. Does each passage portray Guthrie differently? Does Guthrie himself change over time or do the circumstances ?

_____

_____

_____

_____

_____

_____

UNIT 8

COMPOSITION

There are many places in the world today where workers are being oppressed, such as sweatshops in the United States and in the Third World. Yet there is no widespread political movement to protect worker's rights today as there was in the 1930s and 1940s. Why do you think this is? Write an editorial for your school newspaper explaining your perspective. Also, explain to the paper the relevance of the movement to today's world, trying to persuade them to cover the issue more closely.

Use the following table to help you organize your thoughts.

Situation
Cause or Effect
Cause or Effect
Evidence
Evidence
Conclusion:

UNIT 8

EDITING

Read the following passage and determine which word or group of words belongs in each space. Write the letter of the correct answer.

Woody Guthrie _____ for his sardonic humor and direct, to–the–point song
        (1)

writing. He always _____ problems by their names and never skirted issues. In
                (2)

the late 1930s, Guthrie sang on a _____ radio station in Los Angeles. When
                              (3)

people would call in and ask for the words to his songs, _____ a small
                                                      (4)

mimeographed songbook. On the bottom of one page appeared the following:

> This song is Copyrighted in U.S., under Seal of Copyright
> # 154085, for a period of 28 years, and anybody caught singin it
> without our permission, will be mighty good friends of ourn, cause
> we don't give a dern. Publish it. Write it. Sing it. Swing to it. Yodel it.
> We wrote it, that's all we wanted to do. W.G.

____ **1. A** did become famous
     B became famous
     C become famous
     D becoming famous

____ **2. A** identified
     B identify
     C identifying
     D did identified

____ **3. A** progressively
     B progression
     C mostest progressive
     D progressive

____ **4. A** he did mailed out
     B he would mail out
     C he mailing out
     D he was mail out

DISCUSSION QUESTIONS

The focus of this unit is Barbara Jordan's life and political career. To encourage discussion of the topic, ask the following questions:

- What are the some of the differences between American political culture in the 1960s and today?
- People have said that because of Barbara Jordan it is easier for women to serve in politics. Why do you think that is?
- Would you want to be a public servant? Why or why not?

READING—*Using Context Clues*

- When students come across a word they do not recognize, ask them to look at the surrounding words in the sentence for context clues as to the first word's meaning.
- For words that can have more than one meaning, look at the surrounding words in the sentence in order to determine which meaning is being used.

COMPOSITION—*Developing Ideas*

- Ask students to imagine they are running for public office.
- What issues do they need to address?
- What do they want to see changed?
- What special skills do they bring to the job?
- Have students write a speech convincing their classmates to vote for them.

EDITING—*Locating Subjects and Verbs*

Remind students of these guidelines regarding subject and verb:

- A **verb** is a word that shows action (walks, talks, runs) or state of being (is, am, are, was, were, be, being, been).

  EXAMPLE He <u>voted</u> for the Democratic candidate.

- A **subject** is the noun or pronoun that does the action of the verb.

  EXAMPLE She <u>ran</u> for office.

- To find the subject and verb, locate the **action** (verb) first then ask **who** or **what** (subject) performed the action.

  EXAMPLE She won the primary election.
  The **action** is *won*, and the **who** or **what** is *she*.

- Any request or command, such as "Stop" or "Be quiet," has the understood subject *you*.

  EXAMPLE (*You*) Please <u>hand</u> me the paper.

  Hand is the verb. *You* is understood.

BARBARA JORDAN, A BORN LEADER

"One hundred and forty-four years ago, members of the Democratic Party first met in convention to select a Presidential candidate," Texas Congresswoman Barbara Jordan stated in her address to the Democratic National Convention in 1976. ". . . But there is something different about tonight. There is something special about tonight. What is different? What is special? I, Barbara Jordan, am a keynote speaker."

Jordan's life was a series of firsts. She was the first African American to be elected to the Texas Senate in 1966 (against a background of protests and denunciations from some of her male colleagues). In 1972, Barbara Jordan and Andrew Young, of Georgia, became the first African American southerners elected to Congress since Reconstruction in 1883. In 1972, she was elected President *Pro Tempore* of the Senate, and, following Senate tradition, served as Texas governor for a day on June 10, 1972—the first African American woman governor in the history of the United States.

It was her integrity and commitment to political ideals, however, that distinguished Barbara Jordan's career. She gained national attention for her passionate defense of the Constitution during Nixon's impeachment hearings in 1974. Before her colleagues and the American public, Jordan stated, "My faith in the Constitution is whole. It is complete. It is total. I am not going to sit here and be an idle spectator to the diminution, the subversion, the destruction of the Constitution."

Although she retired from public office in 1979, Jordan remained a vital force in national and state politics. She became a professor at the University of Texas-Austin, eventually being appointed LBJ Centennial Chair in National Policy. In 1992, she was again keynote speaker at the Democratic National Convention, and in 1993, President Clinton appointed her Chair of the U.S. Commission on Immigration Reform. In 1994, she received the Presidential Medal of Freedom, the highest award that can be given to a United States civilian.

Jordan suffered from multiple sclerosis for many years, dying on January 17, 1996 at the age of fifty-nine.

As she noted in her 1976 keynote address at the Democratic Convention, "A lot of years passed since 1832, and during that time it would have been most unusual for any national political party to ask that a Barbara Jordan deliver a keynote address . . . but tonight here I am. And I feel that, notwithstanding the past, my presence here is one additional bit of evidence that the American Dream need not forever be deferred."

UNIT 9

A "Stamper and Addresser"

Barbara Jordan was nothing if not pragmatic. A lowly "stamper and addresser" in her early political career, she described the limited opportunities for women in the following manner:

Barbara Jordan receiving the Presidential Medal of Freedom

I had a law degree but no practice, so I went down to Harris County Democratic Headquarters and asked them what I could do. They put me to work licking stamps and addressing envelopes. One night we went out to a church to enlist voters and the woman who was supposed to speak didn't show up. I volunteered to speak in her place and right after that they took me off licking and addressing.

Selected Time Line

1929 — Stock market crashes. Beginning of Great Depression.

1936 — Barbara Charline Jordan born on February 21, in Houston, Texas.

1948 — President Truman issues executive order to desegregate the Armed Forces. Desegregation takes over a decade.

1952 — Jordan graduates high school.

1954 — Supreme Court rules in *Brown vs. The Board of Education* that segregated schools are unconstitutional.

1956 — Jordan graduates magna cum laude from Texas Southern University.

1959 — Jordan graduates from Boston University Law School.

1962 — Jordan runs for the Texas House of Representatives and loses election.

1964 — Jordan runs and loses a second campaign for the Texas legislature.

1965 — Voting Rights Law is passed, ensuring the rights of African Americans to register to vote.

1966 — Jordan is elected to the Texas State Senate and becomes the state's first black senator since 1883.

1968 — Jordan wins a second term in the Texas senate. Students all over America stage protests against Vietnam War and racism.

UNIT 3

1969 — U.S. lands on the moon.

1972 — Jordan is elected to the U.S. House of Representatives and assigned to the House Judiciary Committee.

1973 — Diagnosed with multiple sclerosis that will eventually confine her to a wheelchair.

1974 — Jordan gains national recognition from her televised speech during Nixon's impeachment hearings. Elected to a second term in Congress.

1975 — Jordan expands Voting Rights Act to bring language minorities under the law.

1976 — Jordan delivers keynote speech at Democratic National Convention—wins third congressional term.

1979 — Jordan retires from public life. Becomes professor at the University of Texas-Austin.

1992 — Jordan keynote speaker at Democratic National Convention.

1994 — Jordan receives Presidential Medal of Freedom.

1996 — Jordan dies in Austin, Texas on January 17.

____ **1.** Which word could be substituted for the word <u>pragmatic</u> in the last article without changing the meaning of the sentence?
   A practical
   B outspoken
   C bitter
   D humorless

____ **2.** According to the time-line, which happened first?
   A Voting Rights Law is passed, ensuring the rights of Blacks to register to vote.
   B Jordan receives Presidential Medal of Freedom.
   C U.S. astronauts land on the moon.
   D Supreme Court rules in *Brown vs. The Board of Education* that segregated schools are unconstitutional.

____ **3.** Which sentence BEST reflects the main idea of the second paragraph of the first article?
   A Jordan was the first African American woman to serve in the Texas legislature.
   B Jordan worked hard and succeeded in school.
   C Jordan was an exceptional leader who led a distinguished career.
   D Jordan worked hard for voters' rights.

____ **4.** What first brought Barbara Jordan to national attention?
   A her convictions and ideals
   B her bid for the Texas legislature
   C winning the Presidential Medal for Freedom
   D her televised defense of the Constitution during the Nixon impeachment hearings

5. Based on the time-line, which assumption of the following can be made?

   A Barbara Jordan benefitted from the growing Civil Rights Movement of the 1950s and 1960s.

   B Barbara Jordan preferred her undergraduate studies to her law school studies.

   C Barbara Jordan became discouraged when she lost an election.

   D Barbara Jordan avoided national attention.

6. The author of the first passage probably believes that—

   A Barbara Jordan was an exceptional public servant

   B Barbara Jordan was devoted to her home state of Texas

   C Barbara Jordan was forgotten when she left public service

   D Barbara Jordan encouraged others to be like her

7. After reading the passages, how do you think Jordan felt about being the keynote speaker at the Democratic National Convention in 1972? Explain your answer using what you know from the passage and what you know from your own experience.

_____

_____

_____

_____

_____

_____

_____

_____

_____

_____

_____

8. How does the time-line affect the presentation of Barbara Jordan's life and achievements? Do you find it advantageous or a hindrance to the text?

_____

_____

_____

_____

_____

_____

_____

_____

_____

_____

_____

_____

_____

UNIT

COMPOSITION

Barbara Jordan said, "What the people want is very simple. They want an America as good as its promise."

What do you think of she meant by that? What is the American promise? Why do you think she implied that America was NOT as good as its promise? Write a persuasive essay for your school newspaper in which you agree or disagree with Jordan's statement. Tell what your thoughts are and support them with detailed reasons.

Use the chart below to help you organize your thoughts.

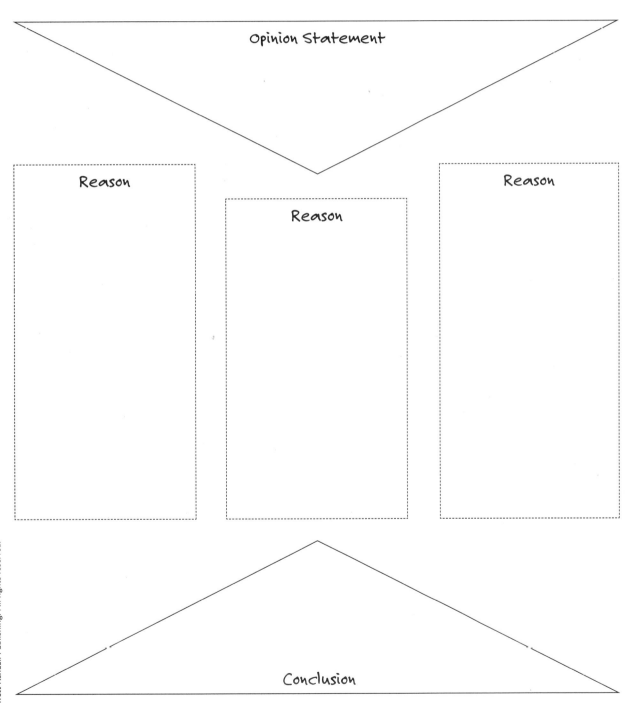

UNIT 9

Read the following. The underlined sections may be one of the following:

Incomplete sentences

Run-on sentences

Correctly written sentences that should be combined

Correctly written sentences that do not need to be re-written

Choose the best way to write each underlined section and mark the letter for your answer.

If the sentence needs no change, mark "Correct as is."

· ·

When I grow up I want to serve in politics like Barbara Jordan she was

(1)

unafraid to stand up for what she believed was right and she encouraged others to

do so too. She was known for her booming voice, her oratorical skills. And her firm

(2)

ethics. Once, when a young man asked her if he should work for her or go to law

(3)

school. She told him to get an education because "you can always work for the

government." She conducted herself with dignity and integrity. Even though

modern students seem to have a lot of cynicism about politics, Barbara Jordan

(4)

insisted that public service is a noble calling. That one person can make a difference.

____ **1. A** Run-on sentence
     B Incomplete sentence
     C Sentences need to be combined
     D Correct as is

____ **3. A** Run-on sentence
     B Incomlete sentence
     C Sentences need to be combined
     D Correct as is

____ **2. A** Run-on sentence
     B Incomplete sentences
     C Sentences need to be combined
     D Correct as is

____ **4. A** Run-on sentence
     B Incomlete sentence
     C Sentences need to be combined
     D Correct as is

TEACHER'S SUGGESTIONS

DISCUSSION QUESTIONS

The focus of this unit is the controversy surrounding Edgar Allan Poe. To encourage discussion of the topic, ask the following questions:

- What do you know about Edgar Allan Poe?
- Why do you think an unflattering but titillating account of Poe's personal life would persist, while other, more sober accounts fail to take hold?
- How much of history is determined by those who write it?

READING—*Recognizing Points of View*

As students read the passages, ask them to think about the following questions:

- Is the primary intent of the author of the passage to inform, to persuade, to express, or to entertain?
- What clues are there in the article which show the author's intent?
- How does the author's perspective affect the style of the text?

COMPOSITION—*Refining Style to Suit Occasion, Audience, and Purpose*

- Ask students to read some of Poe's more well-known stories and poems such as "The Tell Tale Heart" and "The Raven."
- Then ask students to describe how the stories made them feel.
- Have students write a short story or poem that invokes a similar mood.

EDITING—*Using* Comparatives *and* Superlatives

- Comparatives are usually formed by adding *-er* to the end of an adjective.
   EXAMPLE rich + *-er* = richer
   He is richer than she is.
- *The* is placed before a superlative.
   EXAMPLES He is the richest man in the world.
   She is the most beautiful girl in the room.
- A comparative used with *than* compares two people, things, or events.
   EXAMPLE He is richer than Charlotte.
- A comparative can be used with *as* when it compares people, places, things or events about which there is no difference.
   EXAMPLE Kim is beautiful. Rachel is beautiful.
   Kim is *as* beautiful *as* Rachel.

► **READING**

Read the passages "Edgar Allan Poe Is Dead" and "Exquisite Beauty and Strange Proportions," and answer the questions that follow.

EDGAR ALLAN POE IS DEAD

"Edgar Allan Poe is dead. He died in Baltimore the day before yesterday. This announcement will startle many, but few will be grieved by it." This sentence, written by Rufus Wilmot Griswold, appeared in the evening edition of the *New York Tribune*, October 9, 1849. "The poet was known, personally or by reputation, in all this country; he had readers in England, and in several of the states of Continental Europe; but he had few or no friends; and the regrets for his death will be suggested principally by the consideration that in him literary art has lost one of its most brilliant but erratic stars." Thus, in a few words, Griswold initiated one of the more lasting character assassinations in literary history.

Griswold and Poe seemed to dislike each other from the start. Both regarded the other with a mixture of disdain and superiority. Griswold was a former Baptist minister trying his hands at editing, while Poe had already made a name for himself as a fierce and intelligent literary critic. Griswold regarded Poe as his social inferior, an upstart from the South with little education and no legitimate claim on literary criticism. Poe viewed Griswold as a dilettante—a weak writer who was born into prosperity and succeeded on the basis of his social connections rather than his skill. Each represented what the other most despised.

Both were willing to put up an appearance of civility, however, if it benefitted them professionally. From their first meeting in 1841 until Poe's death in 1849, the two men vacillated between veiled civility and outright hostility in their treatment of each other. Griswold quickly discarded all pretenses, however, after Poe's death. He nefariously obtained the rights to Poe's work and began publishing accounts of Poe's life that praised his talent while disparaging his private life. In this way, Griswold gave the appearance of being sympathetic to Poe while sabotaging his character.

He implied that Poe was a lowlife. Sadly, this account of Poe's life remained the only account published for the first thirty years after Poe's death. By the time historians and academics began to look closely at the image of Poe as a brilliant but debauched writer, the slander had imbedded itself in the public consciousness. Even today, the myth persists that Poe's personal corruptions were reflected in his writings.

UNIT 10

EXQUISITE BEAUTY AND STRANGE PROPORTIONS

At West Point there is a gate dedicated to Edgar Allen Poe that sums up his life and work with the following inscription: "There is no exquisite beauty without some strangeness in the proportions."

Of all Poe's poems, it is perhaps his most famous, "The Raven," which best captures the sense of Poe's short and troubled life. The poem describes the author's anguish at the death of his love and his masochistic obsession with a raven he finds in his room. Although the raven can only say one word, "Nevermore," the narrator insists upon asking the bird philosophical questions. The poem ends with an image that is both moving and chilling and captures the urgency, brilliance, and despair that characterized Poe's life:

And the Raven, never flitting, still is sitting, still is sitting
On the pallid bust of Pallas[1] just above my chamber door;
And his eyes have all the seeming of a demon that is dreaming,
And the lamp-light o'er him streaming throws his shadow on the floor,
And my soul from out that shadow that lies floating on the floor
Shall be lifted — nevermore!

[1]Pallas: the Greek goddess of wisdom

____ **1.** Which words could be substituted for <u>slander</u> in the last paragraph of the first passage without changing the meaning of the sentence?
A bad image
B false and malicious statement
C biased viewpoint
D biographical portrait

____ **2.** The author of the first article feels that Edgar Allan Poe—
A was a talented writer who should have been paid more
B was unfairly characterized after his death
C struggled with drugs and alcohol his whole life
D was tormented by psychological demons

____ **3.** According to the second article—
A "The Raven", while popular, is not indicative of Poe's style
B "The Raven" best shows the beauty and despair that characterized Poe's life
C "The Raven" would have made a better inscription on the gate at West Point
D Poe thought "The Raven" was one of his best works

____ **4.** The tone of the first article can best be described as—
A scholarly
B bombastic
C sexist
D childlike

_____ **5.** The purpose of the first article can best be described as—

A to express outrage at the misinformation regarding Edgar Allan Poe

B to explain misinformation regarding Edgar Allan Poe

C to persuade people to read Edgar Allen Poe

D to express concern regarding Edgar Allan Poe's writing

6. After reading the two passages, which view of Poe do you think had a lasting effect on today's readers?

_____

_____

_____

_____

_____

_____

_____

7. In your own words, why do you think the author of the last passage states that the poem "The Raven" best represents Poe's personal life?

_____

_____

_____

_____

_____

_____

_____

_____

_____

_____

UNIT 10

COMPOSITION

To convey a history of a person, event, or place, a writer must research the subject first and then use the writing process to convey what he or she learned or discovered. Often, people who have researched the same subject have completely different conclusions about the subject. Sometimes these conclusions are based on the same facts. Write an essay for your classmates explaining how two people can come to two different conclusions about a subject when their conclusions are based on the same faces. Be sure to organize the details in a logical order, such as cause-and-effect or compare-and-contrast order.

Use the graphic organizer below to organize your ideas.

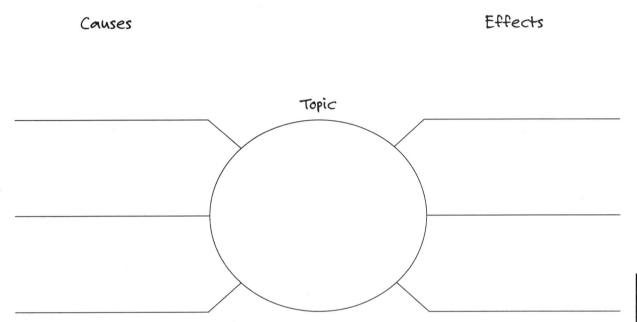

Causes   Effects

Topic

UNIT 10

EDITING

Read the following passage and determine which word or group of words belongs in each space. Write the letter of the correct answer.

Edgar Allan Poe is _____ any American writer. Born Edgar Poe to David and
                              (1)
Elizabeth Poe, both actors, on January 19, 1809, he was the second of three

children. Poe's early childhood reads like one of his _____ stories. His parents,
                                                        (2)
not particularly successful in their chosen profession, lived in poverty. They made

their living performing bit parts in third-rate theatrical companies. By the time Poe

was two years old, his father had disappeared, either dying or abandoning the

family. Elizabeth left her _____ child with relatives and took Edgar and her
                             (3)
infant, Rosalie, with her to Richmond, Virginia. There she suffered the _____
                                                                           (4)
stages of tuberculosis (a common killer of the poor in 19th century America) and

died.

____ **I. A** famousest
       B most famous
       C as famous as
       D as famous

____ **2. A** more melancholy
       B most melancholyest
       C melancholyest
       D much melancholy

____ **3. A** most older
       B oldest
       C most old
       D more older

____ **4. A** last
       B first
       C second
       D beginning

UNIT 10

DISCUSSION QUESTIONS

The focus of this unit is an excerpt from a short story. To encourage discussion of the topic, ask the following questions:

- Have you ever had an anxiety dream? What happened?
- Do your dreams seem real or surreal? Explain.
- Have you ever had an experience where something you thought was one way, but turned out to be another?

READING—*Analyzing Characters*

As students read the passage, ask them to underline details that describe the setting and set the tone. Then ask them to consider the following.

- What does Naho expect to happen in the first paragraph? How do these expectations affect her response?
- What does Naho do in order to calm herself down?
- When does Naho think she is really awake?

COMPOSITION—*Generating Ideas*

- Have students freewrite an interior monologue for Naho. Ask them to imagine what she is thinking and how she feels each time she discovers something different about herself. Have them write for five minutes.
- Have students share any ideas or images that surprised them or were interesting to them in their freewriting.

EDITING—*Identifying Pronouns and Their Antecedents*

- A pronoun is a substitute for a noun. The pronouns or nouns that they refer to are called *antecedents*.

  EXAMPLE *Naho* (antecedent) finished *her* (pronoun) preparations.

- A singular pronoun goes with a singular antecedent and a plural pronoun goes with a plural antecedent.

  EXAMPLE When *debate students* (plural antecedent) argue, *they* (plural pronoun) usually win.

- Indefinite pronouns refer to nonspecific persons or things. They include:

any	each	neither	everyone
either	anybody	someone	none
everything	everybody	anyone	something
no one			

EXAMPLE In debate everyone (singular) performs at *his* or *her* (singular) level of ability.

UNIT 11

PORCINE PROPHECY

Naho looked out of her window. The sun was shining, the birds were singing, and today was going to be the best day of her life. Today was the day of the big debate and she was ready. As ready as she had ever been.

Looking at her feet, Naho discovered to her horror that they had grown twice in size during the night. She couldn't believe it. Was there hair growing on them? Ugly, coarse, bristly black hair? And didn't they look a little bit like hooves? What was going on? What could possibly be happening to her?

At that moment, Naho's mom entered her room. "Hello dear," she said cheerfully. "Today's the big day, huh?"

Naho could not believe that her mother didn't see what was happening to her. "Mom!" she cried, "look at my feet! What's happening? Why are they like this?"

"Why, you're turning into a fat little pig," Naho's mother explained. "Aren't you lucky?"

"MOM!" Naho screamed in panic, "This can't be real!"

"Why, of course it's not," her mother replied, "You're having a nightmare. Relax, the tournament will be fine."

Naho awoke with a start. Relieved that she had only been dreaming, she looked out the window next to her bed. The sun was shining. The birds were singing. It was going to be a great day. It was going to be the day she won the debate!

Cautiously, she peeked under the covers and sneaked a look at her feet. They seemed okay. No hooves. No black, coarse hairs.

Laughing, Naho threw back the covers and shook off her silly dream. She was anxious to get going. The debate competition began at 1:00 and she wanted to go over her notes. Ten different high schools had teams entered in the debate. Only one would win.

She was determined that it was going to be her team.

As she was putting on her robe, she was startled to hear a sort of soft snuffling noise. She paused. Actually, it was more of a grunting than a snuffling. At any rate, it sort of sounded like she was making that noise.

Slowly, her heart full of trepidation, Naho turned and looked into the mirror over her dresser.

Her nose had been replaced with a snout!

"No no no no no no no!" she thought to herself. "This isn't happening. This is just a dream. I'm going to wake myself up and laugh at this."

Naho pinched herself hard and woke up in her bed. "I must really be nervous," she thought. "I've never had a nightmare like that before." She raised her hand and tentatively felt her face. Her small bump of a nose felt just like it always felt. It wasn't a snout, thank goodness.

UNIT 11

"Alright Naho, shake it off." She counseled herself, "It was just a dream. Just a stupid dream."

Rising out of bed, Naho noticed that the weather was gray and overcast. "Well at least that's different." She thought, "I must be awake now."

She looked at her feet. They were the same size seven they had always been. She examined her nose in the mirror. It looked normal.

Just then, her mother opened the door to her room. "Good morning!" she greeted her daughter, "Just wanted to make sure you were up. Today's the big day."

"Mom," Naho asked, "do I look the same to you?"

"Let me see." Her mother replied, looking her over carefully, "No, I can't say as you do."

Naho felt anxiety rise within her. Was she still asleep? She wasn't really turning into a pig, was she?

"You look like the soon-to-be-champion debater of the world." Her mother laughed. "What would you like for breakfast?"

"Definitely *not* bacon," Naho muttered, as she followed her mother out of the room.

____ **1.** Which word could be substituted for the word <u>trepidation</u> without changing the meaning of the sentence?
   A callousness
   B enjoyment
   C dread
   D selfishness

____ **2.** Which one of the following made Naho think she was NOT dreaming?
   A her feet turned into hooves
   B the sun was shining
   C the sky was overcast and gray
   D she heard a snuffling noise

____ **3.** What is the main idea of the story?
   A A girl has a nightmare about turning into a pig.
   B Students who debate suffer a lot of pressure.
   C Bacon is not healthy and shouldn't be eaten.
   D A girl blames debate for a restless night.

____ **4.** Based on the passage, Naho may be best described as—
   A hysterical
   B mean-spirited
   C anxious

   D foolish

____ **5.** The tone of this passage can best be described as—
   A surprising
   B angry
   C joyous
   D bitter

____ **6.** The author probably wrote the story to—
   A entertain readers
   B convince readers
   C persuade readers
   D inform readers

7. What is the tone of the story? How does the author achieve this tone? Use examples from the story.

_____

_____

_____

_____

_____

_____

_____

COMPOSITION

Have you ever had something on your mind and could not think of anything else? Write a humorous essay for your local newspaper or literary magazine describing how this "thing" took control of your life. Why was this thing important to you? How did it disrupt your life? What was the outcome? Be sure to organize your details in a logical order such as sequential order or cause-and-effect order.

Use the questions and the following word web to help you organize your ideas.

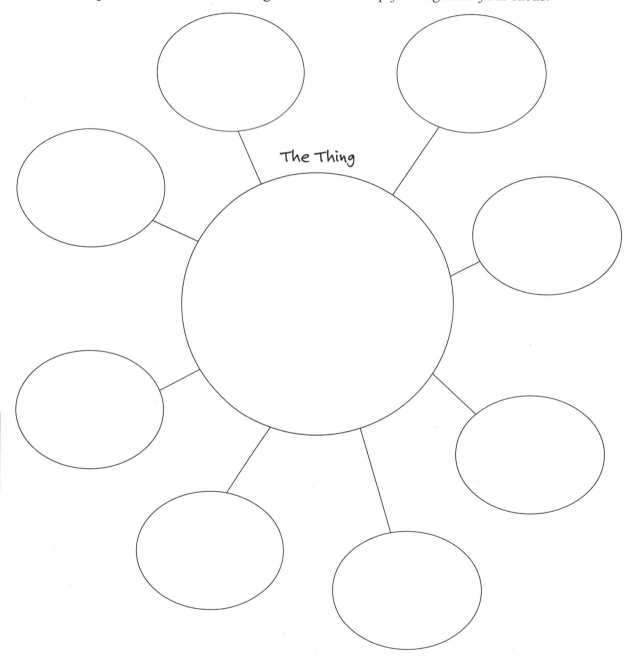

The Thing

UNIT 11

EDITING

Read the following passage and determine the best way to write the underlined sections. If the underlined section does not need to be changed, mark the choice "Correct as is."

Strange beams of light danced upon the surface of Muhammad's desk and the
$\underline{\text{(1)}}$
light had an eerie, greenish glow to it and in fact, seemed to be much more

substantial than mere light. It seemed to be thick, as if it actually had texture. Was

it a person. Taking shape before his eyes? Muhammad watched in fascination as a
$\underline{\text{(2)}}$
being materialized on top of his computer keyboard.

Greetings, earthling! The creature crackled in a strange, computer-sounding
$\underline{\text{(3)}}$
voice.

"Uh . . . greetings?" Muhammad answered uncertainly.
$\underline{\text{(4)}}$

____ **1. A** Strange beams of light danced upon the surface of Muhammad's desk: and the light had an eerie, greenish glow to it and in fact, seemed to be much more substantial than mere light.

B Strange beams of light danced upon the surface of Muhammad's desk. The light had an eerie, greenish glow to it and in fact, seemed to be much more substantial than mere light.

C Strange beams of light danced upon the surface of Muhammad's desk because the light had an eerie, greenish glow to it and in fact, seemed to be much more substantial than mere light.

D Correct as is

____ **2. A** Was it a person taking shape before his eyes?

B Was it a person. Taking shape before his eyes.

C Was it a person; Taking shape before his eyes!

D Correct as is

____ **3. A** "Greetings, earthling!" The creature crackled in a strange, computer-sounding voice.

B Greetings, earthling!; the creature crackled in a strange, computer-sounding voice.

C "Greetings, earthling!" the creature. Crackled in a strange, computer-sounding voice.

D Correct as is

____ **4. A** Uh . . . greetings? Muhammad answered uncertainly.

B "Uh . . . greetings?" Muhammad, answered uncertainly.

C "Uh . . . greetings?" Muhammad—Answered uncertainly.

D Correct as is

UNIT 11

DISCUSSION QUESTIONS

The focus of this unit is Teach For America, an organization that sends recent college graduates to teach in under-funded schools throughout the United States. To encourage discussion of the topic, ask students:

- What are the direst issues facing high-school students today?
- Why do you think some schools are under-funded?
- Why is education important?

READING—*Analyzing Information in a Text*

- Ask students to make a list of the reasons why Teach For America was organized.
- Encourage students to brainstorm their own ideas about possible reasons not mentioned in the passages.
- Work with students to create a list of the benefits to a school that result from Teach For America.

COMPOSITION—*Developing Ideas*

- Ask students to freewrite for five minutes about what they feel is the government's responsibility to the people.
- Then ask students to break off into small groups to discuss their ideas as they apply to education.
- Highlight two viewpoints that arise from the group discussions and stage a debate around these topics.

EDITING—*Recognizing Adverbs*

- An adverb is usually formed by adding -*ly* to an adjective.

Adjective	Adverb
happy	happily
slow	slowly

- Some adverbs have the same form as the adjective.

Adjective	Adverb
fast	fast
late	late
early	early
The hour is late.	He arrived late.
He is a fast worker.	He works fast.

- *Well* is the adverb that corresponds with the adjective *good*.

Adjective	Adverb
She is a good sport.	She responds well.
He is a very good teacher.	He teaches well.

READING

Read the passages "Teach for America," "A Drive to Succeed," and "A Letter Home," and answer the questions that follow.

TEACH FOR AMERICA

Are you ambitious? Driven? A hard worker? Then have I ever got the job for you! Teach For America takes recent college graduates and puts them to work doing the hardest jobs of their lives—teaching kids at under-funded schools.

"My first semester was really difficult," says one Teach For America alumni, "but after a while I grew to love it. It's amazing the growth I saw in my students."

This year, a total of 1,300 recent college graduates will teach in under-served public schools. In a program similar in design to that of the Peace Corps, these "corps" members will spend the next two years devoting their time and energy to teaching students from all walks of life.

Corps members are chosen for a few choice qualities: a passion for challenge, a drive to achieve results, and a commitment to excellence. These young teachers are not only expected to demand the best from their students, but from themselves too.

One corps member teaching in New York City described it this way:

> I had one student. She was really working hard. Really struggling to do the work and do it well. It was heartbreaking because she just wasn't making it. I wanted to reward her effort, but I knew it wouldn't help her unless she could pass the test. After failing the same test for the fifth time, I was on the verge of just passing her. But I knew that wouldn't help her in the long run. I encouraged her to keep at it, and I helped her to understand the mistakes she had made. It took nine attempts in all. But she passed that test. She did it on her own. Now she really has something to be proud of. And I do too.

A DRIVE TO SUCCEED

Teach For America president and founder Wendy Kopp began what would turn out to be her vocation as a thesis project at Princeton. She wanted her thesis to address the inequities in America's education system, but wasn't sure how to do that. She was in a self-proclaimed funk when the idea hit her. Get energetic college graduates to take their enthusiasm and activism into the classroom.

Mere days after her graduation, Kopp was putting her ideas into practice. She wrote letters to

UNIT 12

businesses and others in the philanthropic community to raise money for her dream, and Teach For America was born.

Today Teach For America has an impact on approximately 100,000 children a year. Under-funded schools get trained, enthusiastic teachers in the form of recent college graduates, and the graduates get a life experience that changes them profoundly.

Teach For America takes the best aspects of youth idealism and activism and puts them to work in areas that really need it—America's schools. One reason it has been so successful is that it is so practical. Young people want the world to be a better place. Teach For America provides a venue for them to act upon their beliefs.

A LETTER HOME

Dear Mom and Dad,

Thanks for the care package. I love roasted soybeans. Believe it or not, you can't always find them in the Mississippi Delta.

After a rough first two months, my classes are getting better. It's really shocking to me the circumstances that these kids face every day. I asked one class to list things they were thankful for, and one kid said, "to be alive." I can't even imagine thinking that at thirteen. I took so much for granted.

Even though this is considered a rural environment, those "urban" issues of drugs, poverty, and violence affect my students daily. Last week, two students were shot, one fatally. It has me and the rest of the school pretty depressed.

On the brighter side, my students have been writing the most amazing poetry! It never ceases to amaze me how important writing and literature are in this life. I'll see a student who feels hopeless and defeated find new energy and expression in writing. It is truly inspirational. It becomes imperative to me that my students understand that their thoughts and lives matter. They can conquer even the most abysmal circumstances through their determination and will. It's hard to imagine needing that much commitment just to get through life, but that's just what these kids ARE going to need if they want to escape the traps of poverty and indifference. It is so incredible to watch these kids get excited when they are actually using their brains!

I know life is hard and that everybody struggles. I'm just so happy to be doing something that I love so passionately. It means a lot to make a difference.

That's all for now. Send more soybeans!

Love,
Roberto

____ **1.** Which one of the following sentences BEST summarizes the main idea of the first passage?

A Teach For America is a philanthropic organization.

B Teach For America recruits ambitious, hard working college graduates to work in under-funded schools.

C Teach For America is working to change the educational system.

D Teach For America operates in most American cities.

____ **2.** Teach For America was created because—

A a group of students wanted to improve the educational system

B schools recruited recent college graduates to help teach students

C Wendy Kopp thought of it as her thesis project

D the government cut funds for education

____ **3.** Which one of the following best defines the meaning of the word imperative in the last passage?

A impossible

B important

C necessary

D clear

____ **4.** Which one of the following statements represents a fact?

A My students have been writing the most amazing poetry!

B Young people want the world to be a better place.

C Wendy Kopp wanted her thesis to address the inequities in America's education system.

D Teach For America takes the best aspects of youth idealism and activism and puts them to work in areas that really need it.

____ **5.** Teach For America is effective because—

A it gets funded by business and philanthropists

B it is a practical organization that provides a venue for activism

C it gets college graduates to teach for very little money

D it is affiliated with the Peace Corps

____ **6.** The second passage argues that Wendy Kopp—

A waited a year after graduating before she started Teach For America

B believed that getting enthusiastic college graduates to teach would help address inequities in the educational system

C wanted to volunteer her time for a good cause

D developed the concept of Teach For America as her thesis at Harvard

7. Use facts from the articles to support the following statement:

Young people want the world to be a better place. Teach For America provides a venue for them to act upon their beliefs.

_____

_____

_____

_____

8. Describe the writing style of the three passages. How does each style contribute to the writer's overall intention in writing the passages?

_____

_____

_____

_____

UNIT 12

COMPOSITION

Many people in America are in need of financial assistance in order to receive a college education. What responsibility, if any, do you think the U.S. Government has to these individuals? Write an essay explaining your thoughts to your classmates, and be sure to back up your view with supporting evidence.

Use the following table to help you organize your ideas.

Opinion Statement:	
Advantages:	Disadvantages
Conclusion:	

UNIT 12

EDITING

Read the following passage and determine which word or group of words belongs in each space. Write the letter of the correct answer.

New corps members _____ an intensive five-week training program where
      (1)

they gain experience teaching while receiving guidance from veteran educators.

They _____ to one of thirteen sites where school districts hire and pay them as
      (2)

regular beginning teachers. Local offices _____ corps members to their new
                                          (3)

schools and communities and foster professional and personal support networks.

Teach For America _____ to places as diverse as Houston, Texas to rural
                        (4)

Louisiana and New York City. In its support and its educational mission, it is truly an

exceptional program.

____ **1. A** undergo
       B underwent
       C undergoed
       D did underwent

____ **2. A** was then assigned
       B are then assign
       C is then assigned
       D are then assigned

____ **3. A** helping orient
       B help orienting
       C help orient
       D helped orient

____ **4. A** sending corps members
       B sends corps members
       C sent corps members
       D did sends corps members

UNIT 12

DISCUSSION QUESTIONS

The focus of this unit is the myth of the golden apple that started the Trojan War. To encourage discussion of the topic, ask the following questions:

- What purpose do you think myths serve in a society?

- What are some modern day myths?

- The ancient Greeks felt that the gods toyed with men and suffered human emotions such as jealousy and envy. How do you think these beliefs about gods helped the ancient Greeks to understand their world?

READING—*Summarizing*

As students read the passage, ask them to do the following:

- List the events in the passage.

- Note how the order of the events determines the outcome.

- Summarize the main idea behind the myth of the golden apple.

COMPOSITION—*Generating Ideas*

Ask students to brainstorm a list of myths (such as Cinderella, Johnny Appleseed, Paul Bunyan, George Washington and the cherry tree, etc. . .) Then ask them to describe one myth keeping these questions in mind:

- What is _____ similar to? In what ways?

- What is _____ different from? In what ways?

- How does _____ make me feel?

EDITING—*Using The Articles* A *and* An *Correctly*

- Use *a* before a noun or adjective that does not start with a vowel sound (*a, e, i, o, u* or *y*).

  EXAMPLES Paris saw *a* goddess appear.
  She was carrying *a* beautiful shield.

- Use *an* before a noun or adjective that begins with a vowel sound.

  EXAMPLES Paris took *an* apple.
  Zeus told Paris he had *an* hour to decide.

UNIT 13

READING

Read the passage "The Golden Apple," and answer the questions that follow.

THE GOLDEN APPLE

Many people have heard of the Trojan War and Helen of Troy and the "face that launched a thousand ships," but how many know of the golden apple?

In Homer's *Iliad*, the golden apple is the domino that, once knocked down, started the ten years of war between the Greeks and the Trojans. It all began when the goddess Eris, also known as Discord, was not invited to a wedding that all the other gods on Mount Olympus were attending. Rather than pitching a terrible fit, she sent a golden apple. It was the most beautiful apple any of the other gods and goddesses had seen. On the apple ran an inscription—"For the Fairest."

Discord may not have thrown a temper tantrum, but she knew what she was doing. Suddenly, the entire wedding was in disarray as every goddess in the room attempted to claim what she felt belonged to herself. Hera, queen of the gods; Athene, the goddess of wisdom; Aphrodite, goddess of love; Demeter, the goddess of fertility; and all the Graces—each in her own fashion was beautiful beyond compare. Soon the wedding was in complete chaos as each god and goddess supported his or her favorite candidate.

Years passed and the debate raged on. The gods narrowed it down to Hera, Athene, and Aphrodite. Between splendor, wisdom, and woman's loveliness, they could not choose. Finally, out of fatigue, the gods decided that an impartial judge was necessary to settle the matter. They agreed to select a mortal man who knew nothing of the goddesses. For this purpose, the gods choose the young shepherd Paris.

Paris had a story of his own. Before he was born, his mother, Queen Hecuba, had a terrible dream. She dreamt that her unborn boy was no boy at all but a terrible flame that would destroy the city. Her husband, King Priam, upon hearing the soothsayers confirm that this was indeed a bad omen, ordered his son killed rather than risk his kingdom. Before the king's order could be obeyed, however, some poor shepherds took pity on Paris and adopted him as their own. A beautiful and peaceful child, Paris grew up in sight of his father's city but had no knowledge of his high birth.

Enter the gods. Attracted by Paris' beauty and innocence, they sent him the apple and instructed him to settle their quandary. The three goddesses appeared to him in a glade and bade him decide who was the fairest.

You can imagine what poor Paris felt when faced with the heavenly beauty of those goddesses. He didn't know what to think. Hera promised to make him king of everything. Athene guaranteed him all the wisdom known to man. But it was Aphrodite, with her heavy scent of narcissi and daffodils that drew Paris to her. She laughed gaily and whispered in his ear, "You shall have the fairest woman in the world as your wife."

Paris handed her the apple.

Aphrodite was victorious and the other goddesses were enraged. But Aphrodite didn't abandon Paris after he picked her to be the fairest of the fair. She told him of his birth, led him into Troy, and caused Hecuba and

Priam to disregard their fears and accept him as their son. She also repeated her promise that he would have the most beautiful wife.

The rest is history. Helen of Sparta was the most beautiful woman in the world. But unfortunately, she already had a husband. Paris abducted her and thus began the Trojan War. Aphrodite never said getting the most beautiful woman in the world as a wife was going to be easy.

____ **1.** Which word could be substituted for the word <u>abducted</u> in the last paragraph without changing the meaning of the sentence?

A killed

B married

C kidnapped

D marked

____ **2.** Which one of the following was NOT offered to Paris?

A earthly wisdom

B a kingdom

C the most beautiful woman as his wife

D power of the gods

____ **3.** What is the main idea of the second paragraph?

A Eris, upset that she was not invited to a wedding, sent a golden apple to cause strife amongst the gods.

B The ancient Greeks used mythology as a means of understanding the world in which they lived.

C King Priam ordered that Paris be killed.

D Every goddess at the wedding thought she should be called the fairest.

____ **4.** Based on the passage, Paris can be BEST described as:

A beautiful but naive

B peaceful and humane

C innocent and beautiful

D argumentative and angry

____ **5.** The tone of this passage can BEST be described as—

A serious

B ironic

C religious

D cutting

____ **6.** Which one of the following is an opinion stated in the passage?

A Helen of Sparta was the most beautiful woman in the world.

B Aphrodite told Paris of his birth.

C Eris sent a golden apple to the wedding.

D Paris was taken in by shepherds.

7. After reading the passage, what message do you think this myth served in ancient Greece? Explain your answer using examples from the passage and what you know from your own experience.

_____

_____

_____

_____

_____

_____

_____

_____

_____

_____

UNIT 13

COMPOSITION

Myths and legends have been passed down through the ages. Some have been recorded in writing, and others are part of some cultures' oral traditions. Write an essay for your school's literary magazine explaining the purpose and importance of myths and legends in our society. Use facts and examples to support your opinions. Be sure to organize your details in a logical order.

Use the cluster diagram below to generate and organize your ideas.

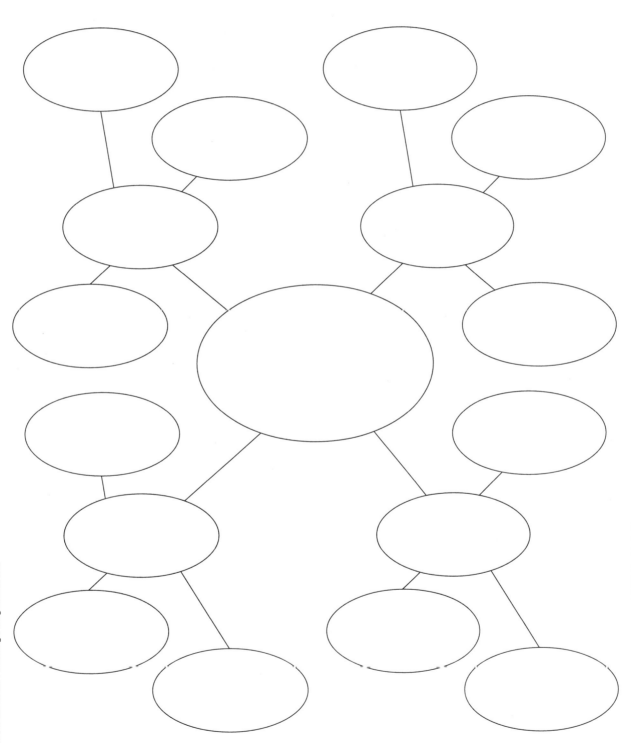

UNIT 13

EDITING

Read the following passage. The underlined sections may be one of the following:

Run-on sentence

Correctly written sentences that should be combined

Correctly written sentences that do not need to be re-written

Choose the best way to write each underlined section and mark the letter for your answer. If the sentence needs no change, mark "Correct as is."

....

(1) American myths like Johnny Appleseed help foster the idea that America is a land of democracy, opportunity, and plenty the real Johnny Appleseed was actually John Chapman. **(2)** He lived during the end of the 18th century. And the beginning of the 19th century. He really did go West and plant a bunch of apple trees. **(3)** In the myth, however, he plants apple trees everywhere so that no one would go hungry. In reality, he planted seeds because the law required that each settler plant fifty apple trees during their first year in order to ensure stability for the new homesteads. **(4)** John Chapman owned many tracts of land throughout Ohio and Indiana. And sold (and sometimes gave) apple seeds and seedlings to settlers.

____ **1. A** American myths like Johnny Appleseed help foster the idea that America is a land of democracy, opportunity, and plenty. The real Johnny Appleseed was actually John Chapman.

    B American myths like Johnny Appleseed help foster the idea that America is a land of democracy, opportunity, and plenty, the real Johnny Appleseed was actually John Chapman.

    C American myths like Johnny Appleseed help foster the idea that America is a land of democracy. Opportunity and plenty. The real Johnny Appleseed was actually John Chapman.

    D Correct as is

____ **2. A** He lived during the end of the 18th century; And the beginning of the 19th century.

    B He lived during the end of the 18th century—and the beginning of the 19th century.

    C He lived during the end of the 18th century and the beginning of the 19th century.

    D Correct as is

____ **3. A** In the myth—however—he plants apple trees everywhere so that no one would go hungry.

    B In the myth however he plants apple trees everywhere so that no one would go hungry.

    C In the myth: however, he plants apple trees everywhere so that no one would go hungry.

    D Correct as is

____ **4. A** John Chapman owned many tracts of land throughout Ohio and Indiana and sold (and sometimes gave) apple seeds and seedlings to settlers.

    B John Chapman owned many tracts of land throughout Ohio and Indiana thus sold (and sometimes gave) apple seeds and seedlings to settlers.

    C John Chapman owned many tracts of land throughout Ohio and Indiana selling (and sometimes gave) apple seeds and seedlings to settlers.

    D Correct as is

▷ **DISCUSSION QUESTIONS**

The focus of this unit is a personal narrative about the parent/child relationship. To encourage discussion of the topic, ask the following questions:

- Do you find it easy to tell your parents or guardians what you really think?
- How important is it to you to please your parents or guardians?
- What role does your parents' or guardians' beliefs have in shaping your own beliefs?

▷ **READING**—*Analyzing Information*

As students read the passage, ask them to consider the following questions.

- What does the title tell me about the passage?
- What is the action of the passage?
- How does the narrator feel about the information being given?
- What are the important details in the passage?

▷ **COMPOSITION**—*Responding Appropriately to a Given Topic*

Ask students to consider a time when they either agreed or disagreed emphatically with a parent or guardian. Then ask:

- IIow would I prcscnt this cvcnt to a group of people my parents' or guardians' age?
- How would I present this event to a group of people my own age?
- How would I present this event to a group of children?

▷ **EDITING**—*Correcting Sentence Fragments*

- A sentence fragment is a group of words that does not express a complete thought.
  EXAMPLE Riding across the bridge.
  The dog on the long leash.
- To check for fragments, make sure a subject and predicate, or subject and verb can be identified in each sentence.
  EXAMPLE The golf ball (subject) is waffled (predicate).
  The golf ball (subject) soared (verb) over the sand pit.

UNIT 14

READING

Read the passage "Golf, My Dad, and My Two Left Feet," and answer the questions that follow.

GOLF, MY DAD, AND MY TWO LEFT FEET

I was never much of an athlete and I think this was a huge disappointment to my father. He was an amazing basketball player. He went to college on a basketball scholarship and was even recruited to play professional ball. All his life he played a sport of some kind, and in his face I saw a desire for me to do the same.

Rather than possessing incredible athletic acumen like my dad, however, I was born with two left feet, and two left hands, as well. I never had the agility, the stamina, or the determination it takes to be good at sports. Basketballs would hit me. Baseballs avoided my bat. Soccer balls slipped by my feet. Forget that. I wanted dance lessons.

Yes, dance lessons . . . I wanted to tap and twirl and glide and swing. Instead I got baseball, basketball, soccer, and golf. Golf? Who wants to play golf? Not me.

But that's what I got and that's where I dutifully tried to excel. I would swing with all my might at the ball, look out into space where I imagined it was gracefully arching toward the green, and then realize with chagrin that I hadn't hit it at all. There was the white ball, sitting on the tee, mocking me.

To make matters worse, we didn't have a lot of money. Going on the course was my dad's special treat to me. Every time we went to the golf course, I felt I was flushing money down the toilet.

I would try harder. I would swing with all of my might. I would concentrate, focus, think Zen, and creatively visualize the ball flying hundreds of yards. But try as I might, I just didn't have the touch.

Once I even broke a club. It was a beautiful day. The sky was blue, the grass was green, and everywhere, golfers were enjoying their game. "Stupid game," I muttered as I missed yet again. "Stupid, stupid game." No one was ever rude to me or taunted me for my lack of prowess on the course. Somehow I thought it would have been better if they had teased me. I would have had someone or something to blame. I would have had an excuse of some sort. But no, everyone was very supportive and encouraging. "You can do it." "Keep trying." "Follow through. That's it."

I didn't mean to break the club. It just slipped out of my hand after a particularly energetic swing. Sure, I was a little close to the tree. But I have to admit, though, as the club wrapped itself around the trunk, my heart did a furtive, joyful leap.

My father looked at me closely before resting his hand heavily on my shoulder. "I just don't think this game is for you." I became preoccupied with examining my shoelaces.

Gee, Dad, really?

I love my father and now almost am able to laugh with him about my lack of sports skill.

UNIT 14

It seems he was just trying to get me excited about the things that excited him. I *was* excited about stuff, but it just happened to be different stuff than my dad. He never actually pressured me, per se, but it wasn't until I was able to talk to him about my wanting to please him (and feeling like a dope when I failed) that things improved between us.

Now, instead of me trying to be good at things that my father was good at, I just try to be good at being myself. I'd still like to dance, but sadly, my left feet followed me to the dance floor. My dad and I don't golf together anymore, thank goodness, but we do lots of other things together. I've learned that what I wanted—to be myself—is what pleased him all along.

____ **1.** In the passage the word <u>preoccupied</u> means—

    A not being occupied

    B already occupied

    C after being occupied

    D before becoming occupied

____ **2.** Which one of the following was NOT a reason the narrator did not enjoy sports?

    A She had two left feet.

    B She did not have the agility, stamina, or determination needed to be good at sports.

    C She had a painful knee injury.

    D She wanted to dance.

____ **3.** What is the main idea of the passage?

    A Being herself and communicating her feelings allowed the narrator and her father to truly enjoy and appreciate each other.

    B One should always do what our parents want us to do, regardless.

    C The narrator wishes her father had not wasted money trying to teach her to play golf.

    D Her father and she can't talk because she hates golf.

____ **4.** The narrator's father wanted the narrator to play golf because—

    A he wanted the narrator to play golf professionally

    B he enjoyed playing golf

    C he thought golf taught good social skills

    D he had a lot of money and didn't mind wasting it

____ **5.** How did the narrator feel when the golf club broke?

    A secretly pleased

    B embarrassed

    C regretful

    D overjoyed

____ **6.** The narrator probably wrote this passage in order to—

    A entertain and inform the reader about parent-child relationships

    B entertain the reader about a time in her life

    C inform the reader about the hardships of golf

    D persuade the reader to play sports with his/her parent

7. Why was the narrator sarcastic after the golf club broke?

_____

_____

_____

_____

_____

_____

COMPOSITION

Is there any time in your life when you felt you were doing something for someone other than yourself? How did this make you feel? Write an essay from your class explaining your experience and informing them of the reasons you felt compelled to participate. Also, explain how you felt during the activity, and what effect, if any, his experience had on you. Be sure to organize details in a logical order such as sequential order.

Use the organizer below to help you organize your thoughts.

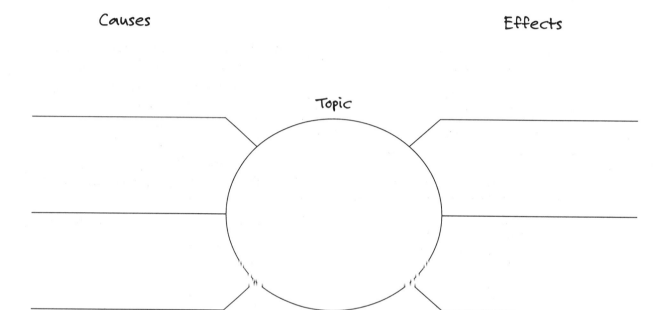

Causes

Effects

Topic

UNIT 14

EDITING

Read the following passage and determine which word or group of words belongs in each space. Write the letter of the correct answer.

One time I was playing baseball with my father and I overheard him _____ a
(1)
friend of his that I swung like a girl. I was so mad at him I didn't know what to say
and _____ hardly believe he had said it. I *am* a girl, but I sure did not like the
(2)
insult implied by saying that I *swung* like a girl. I don't think my dad _____ it,
(3)
but he offended me greatly that day. It is not OK to denigrate people because of
their sex, race, religion, or *any* reason for that matter. When I asked my father what
he meant by that comment, he _____ that he didn't mean anything negative by it.
(4)
He probably didn't, still, it's always important to think before speaking, even if you
are the father. Words can hurt.

____ **1. A** tell
     B telled
     C told
     D did tell

____ **2. A** couldn't
     B can't
     C could
     D could not

____ **3. A** did realize
     B realizing
     C realize
     D realized

____ **4. A** tried says
     B tried to say
     C trying to say
     D try to said

DISCUSSION QUESTIONS

The focus of this unit is an overview of the agricultural, industrial, and technological revolutions. To encourage discussion of the topic, ask the following questions:

- What are some of the changes that resulted from the switch from a hunter-gatherer culture to an agricultural culture?
- What are some of the changes that occurred in the switch from an agricultural to an industrial society?
- What were some of the benefits of a hunter-gatherer society?

READING—*Identifying Supporting Ideas*

As students read the first passage, ask them to consider:

- What do the titles reveal about the passages?
- What are the main ideas of the passages?
- How are those ideas supported?

COMPOSITION—*Developing Ideas*

Ask students to consider what life was like for people experiencing the transition to either an agricultural society or an industrial society. Then ask them to consider:

- What might _____ have felt like?
- Have I ever experienced anything like _____ ?
- What might I have thought about_____ ?
- What major transitions have I experienced?

EDITING—*Clauses*

- A *subject* is the noun or noun phrase that is the doer of the action of a sentence.
  EXAMPLE *William* opened the factory door.
- A *predicate* modifies the subject and includes the verb, objects, or phrases governed by the verb.
  EXAMPLE William *opened the factory door.*
- *Clauses* are groups of words with a subject and predicate.
- A *main clause* stands alone as a sentence.
- A *subordinate clause* is incomplete and is used with a main clause to express an idea.
  EXAMPLE I like working at a computer (main clause) when I have time (subordinate clause).

READING

Read the passages "A Sedentary Revolution," "A Manufactured Revolution," and "A Desktop Revolution," and answer the questions that follow.

A SEDENTARY REVOLUTION

Historians argue that there are only two revolutions in the history of humankind that matter: the Agricultural Revolution and the Industrial Revolution. The Agricultural Revolution occurred over 9,000 years ago and had an impact on humankind and nature that is so vast that it can be difficult to imagine. Early humans were hunter-gatherers. They followed herds of animals for food and gathered what plants were available. They were on the move daily. This meant that they had no need for wealth, extra possessions, written language, or breakable items such as pottery. They had no need for cities, as everything they used was carried on their backs.

When humans first began to cultivate plants and animals, they radically altered the nature of their existence. Living in one spot permanently meant a sedentary lifestyle based on exploiting a relatively small amount of land very intensively (rather than exploiting a large amount of land extensively) over a long period of time. Raising crops meant that there was a surplus of food that then needed to be stored. This necessitated the creation of buildings. It also created the notion of wealth, because for the first time it was reasonable to acquire objects and keep them.

Wealth brought with it the need for protection. Ancient societies built walled cities to protect their supplies from marauders. Constructing buildings required cooperation, organization, and management—i.e., government. Once communities were organized in this way it greatly expanded what humans could accomplish. At the same time this new mode of life permanently altered the ancient egalitarianism of hunter-gatherer societies. Life in towns and cities required a new mode of social organization—a division between those who direct and manage and those who are directed. As specializations emerged in the economy, inequalities of wealth and status emerged with them. Hierarchies of wealth, status, and power characterized new societies.

A MANUFACTURED REVOLUTION

Between 1750 and 1850 in Europe, Asia, and America, another great revolution occurred. After thousands of years of being agriculturally based,

societies changed, in the course of a century, to a manufacturing base. Inventions and new technology resulted in the factory system of large-scale machine production and greater economic specialization. The laboring class, formerly dispersed and employed mostly in agriculture, began to become centralized in giant urban factory centers.

During this time, canals, railroads, and roads were built to facilitate the

UNIT 15

transportation of goods to markets. New inventions made it possible for more work to be done more quickly. Suddenly, a job that used to take many workers days or even weeks to finish could be done in hours by a machine.

One of the biggest impacts of the industrial revolution was the change in how societies operated. Rather than being centered on the home and village, work became centered on factories. Women and children, who traditionally picked up extra income by doing piecework at home, suffered disproportionately when work was taken to the factories. One report, circa 1794, stated:

> The . . . men and boys may possibly turn to some other work, but it is not so with the wife and daughters of the day-laborers, whose occupation in a country parish where no particular manufactory is carried on, must be within their own dwelling; who deprived of Woollen Spinning have no other employment, (except when they can go into the fields) to bring in any money towards the support of the Family.

With work being centered in urban cities, the small villages and countryside soon fell into economic hardship. The Industrial Revolution changed the face of nations, providing the economic base for population expansion and improvement in living standards. But it also created a host of problems, including labor-management conflicts, worker boredom, and environmental pollution.

A DESKTOP REVOLUTION

Many scholars argue that humankind is once again in the throes of a revolution. Like the Agricultural Revolution and the Industrial Revolution before it, this new revolution is based on new technology. The personal computer and the Internet are the vanguards of this revolution. Individual citizens have access to greater information and resources. The desktop computer has changed the way economies function. The Internet and improvements in transportation have expanded local markets into global markets.

Like the revolutions that preceded it, the Technological Revolution brings changes that are both positive and negative. New markets have resulted in new wealth on unprecedented levels. But in the United States, the majority of that wealth rests solidly with the top fifth of the population. The bottom quintile in America has actually seen wages and wealth decrease. So while there is a perception that everyone is benefitting from the growing economy, certain groups are actually suffering setbacks.

Change is impossible to stop. But the manner in which societies manage change can be controlled. In coping with the Technological Revolution, it is imperative that societies protect the welfare of all citizens while, at the same time, continue to work towards a future that develops and embraces new technologies.

____ **1.** In the last article, the word <u>unprecedented</u> means—

    A occurring before

    B never having occurred

    C almost occurring

    D about to occur

____ **2.** Which one of the following did NOT result from the Agricultural Revolution?

    A cities

    B written language

    C the notion of wealth

    D nomadic culture

____ **3.** Which sentence BEST reflects the main idea of the first paragraph of the last passage?

    A Many experts feel that society is currently undergoing a technological revolution.

    B The Technological Revolution has resulted in inequalities in the distribution of wealth.

    C The Technological Revolution brings positive and negative changes.

    D Progress is impossible to stop.

____ **4.** Based on the second passage, the Industrial Revolution can best be described as—

    A an event that changed the face of societies

    B an event that created huge amounts of capital for a select group of people

    C a huge improvement in how societies were organized

    D an event that provided the economic base for population expansion and improvement in living standards but also created problems

____ **5.** Based on the second passage, which of the following probably did NOT result from the Industrial Revolution?

    A workers' unions

    B environmental pollution

    C child labor laws

    D small villages

____ **6.** The author of these articles probably wrote them in order to:

    A inform readers

    B entertain readers

    C persuade readers

    D frighten readers

7. Why do you think the first article is titled "A Sedentary Revolution"?

_____

_____

_____

_____

_____

_____

_____

_____

8. Based on the articles, which revolution do you think had the biggest impact on society? Why?

_____

_____

_____

_____

_____

_____

_____

_____

_____

UNIT 15

COMPOSITION

Do you agree that the world is presently going through a major revolution, the Technological Revolution? Are computers merely tools for the individual, or do they affect the way we function as a society? Write an essay for a scholarly journal discussing your view. Be sure to organize your details in a logical order.

Use the chart below to help you organize your thoughts.

Situation

Cause or Effect   Cause or Effect   Cause or Effect

Evidence

Conclusion

EDITING

Read the following passage and determine which type of error, if any, appears in the underlined section. Write the letter of the correct answer.

Human communities are ingenious at finding ways to adapt to the limitations
(1)
in food sources; Humans need twelve amino acids to survive and reproduce. Cereal

grains only provide adequate quantities of too of the twelve amino acids. Cultures
(2)
that lived mainly on grains, like those of Europe, the Middle East, and Asia,

supplemented their diet with animal protein from milk, meat, fish, or soybeans.

The Ancient Cultures of the Americas, unlike those of Europe and Asia, did not use
(3)
large domestic animals. This is because their mane food—plants, corn, squash, and
(4)
beans—provide all twelve of the necessary amino acids.

_____ **1. A** Spelling error
      B Capitalization error
      C Punctuation error
      D No error

_____ **2. A** Spelling error
      B Capitalization error
      C Punctuation error
      D No error

_____ **3. A** Spelling error
      B Capitalization error
      C Punctuation error
      D No error

_____ **4. A** Spelling error
      B Capitalization error
      C Punctuation error
      D No error

Answer Key

UNIT 1

Reading *(page 4)*

1. B	**3.** A	**5.** B
2. D	**4.** C	**6.** B

7. Possible response: People should be allowed to hike in bear country only if they have educated themselves about bears.

8. Possible response: "Frenzied Grizzly" sensationalized the event of the hiker being killed and presented the bear as a crazed predator. "Mother Murdered" victimized the bear but presented a more complex picture of the interaction between bears and humans.

Composition *(page 5)*

Answers will vary but should include facts, examples, and reasons to support opinions.

Editing *(page 6)*

1. A	**2.** C	**3.** C	**4.** B

UNIT 2

Reading *(page 9)*

1. A	**3.** A	**5.** A
2. D	**4.** C	**6.** C

7. Possible response: Alexie challenges traditional images of American Indians by writing modern characters facing modern problems.

Composition *(page 10)*

Responses will vary but should include examples and reasons to support connections that the students make between themselves and a work of fiction or poetry.

Editing *(page 11)*

1. A	**2.** C	**3.** B	**4.** D

UNIT 3

Reading *(page 15)*

1. D	**3.** A	**5.** A
2. B	**4.** B	**6.** B

7. Possible response: I would need to get access to a submersible and camera. I would need to go to an area where warm and cold water currents converge because there I would have the best chances of sighting a giant squid.

8. Possible response: Giant squids are interesting to scientists because no one has ever seen one in its natural habitat. Giant squid live all over the world's oceans but so far, no attempt to observe a giant squid in the deep ocean has been successful. Scientists use many different tools to try and view giant squid. No one is certain why giant squid attack whales and ships. Some people think they are attacking to get food. Other people think that the squid get pushed up into warm waters and attach themselves to boats and whales because they are trying to get back to colder, deeper waters.

Composition *(page 16)*

Answers will vary but should include facts, examples, and reasons to support opinions.

Editing *(page 17)*

1. A	**2.** B	**3.** B	**4.** D

UNIT 4

Reading *(page 20)*

1. C	**3.** A	**5.** A
2. C	**4.** C	**6.** C

7. Responses should include the author's list of positive results from her vacation and her lifelong enjoyment of them. Responses might also mention student's appreciation of learning something positive from a seemingly negative experience.

Composition *(page 21)*

Responses will vary but should include effective details that support the main idea of the essays.

Editing *(page 22)*

1. A	**2.** C	**3.** C	**4.** A

UNIT 5

Reading *(page 26)*

1. D	**3.** A	**5.** D
2. C	**4.** A	**6.** A

7. Responses will vary but should mention that Shackleton overcame many obstacles and that all of his crew survived the expedition. Responses might also mention student's experience of overcoming obstacles.

8. Response will very but should include examples from the text to support the students' answer.

Composition (page 27)

Responses will vary but should include facts, examples, and reasons to support opinions.

Editing (page 28)

1. B   **2.** A   **3.** A   **4.** C

UNIT 6

Reading (pages 31–32)

1. C   **3.** D   **5.** A
2. B   **4.** A   **6.** B

7. Responses should include information about the rise in sports salaries and ticket costs. Responses might also note the relatively low pay of public servants and educators in comparison to sports stars.

8. Responses should note differences in the tone of each article. The first article is not critical of the amount of money being spent while the second article is.

Composition (page 33)

Responses will vary but should include facts, examples, and reasons to support opinions.

Editing (page 34)

1. B   **2.** A   **3.** D   **4.** D

UNIT 7

Reading (page 37)

1. C   **3.** A   **5.** A
2. C   **4.** C   **6.** A

7. Responses should mention that the anticipation and effort leading up to the trip and the decision to hate it because of the cold.

Composition (page 38)

Answers will vary but should include facts, examples, and reasons to support the students' opinions.

Editing (page 39)

1. B   **2.** C   **3.** A   **4.** B

UNIT 8

Reading (page 43)

1. B   **3.** D   **5.** C
2. A   **4.** A   **6.** C

7. Responses should cite Guthrie's travelling and days as a migrant worker. They should also cite his support of and identification with migrant workers and workers' rights

8. Responses should cite Steinbeck's reference to Guthrie as someone who endures and fights against oppression. They should also mention the hardships suffered by Americans during the Depression and Dust Bowl years.

Composition (page 44)

Responses will vary but should include facts, examples, and reasons to support opinions.

Editing (page 45)

1. B   **2.** A   **3.** D   **4.** B

UNIT 9

Reading (pages 49–50)

1. A   **3.** C   **5.** A
2. D   **4.** D   **6.** A

7. Responses will vary but should mention Jordan's references to racial exclusion and her optimism that eventually all citizens could share in the American dream of equality.

8. Responses should might point out that the timeline presents information in a way that is easy to read and reference.

Composition (page 51)

Responses will vary but should include facts, examples, and reasons to support opinions.

Editing (page 52)

1. A   **2.** C   **3.** B   **4.** B

UNIT 10

Reading (pages 55–56)

1. B   **3.** B   **5.** B
2. B   **4.** A

6. Responses might include information from Griswold's comments and/or Poe's history of drinking.

7. Responses should note the sense of urgency and despair in the writing.

Composition (page 57)

Responses will vary but should include facts, examples, and reasons to support opinions.

Editing (page 58)

1. C   **2.** A   **3.** B   **4.** A

UNIT 11

Reading (page 61)

1. C   **3.** A   **5.** A
2. C   **4.** C   **6.** A

7. Possible response: The tone story is humorous. The author achieves the tone by the manner in which the author reveals what happens to Naho the day of the debate.

Composition (page 62)

Responses will vary but should include details that support the main idea of the personal narrative. The details should be organized in logical order.

Editing (page 63)

1. B   **2.** A   **3.** A   **4.** D

UNIT 12

Reading (page 67)

1. B   **3.** C   **5.** B
2. C   **4.** C   **6.** B

7. Responses should cite examples from the articles that illustrate how Teach For America corps members feel gratified with their work.
8. Responses will vary but should include facts and examples that support opinions.

Composition (page 68)

Responses will vary but should include facts, examples, and reasons to support opinions.

Editing (page 69)

1. A   **2.** D   **3.** C   **4.** B

UNIT 13

Reading (page 72)

1. C   **3.** A   **5.** B
2. D   **4.** C   **6.** A

7. Possible responses should mention Eris's being unhappy at being shunned (never offend an important person) and Paris'

susceptibility to physical beauty (beauty may lead people astray).

Composition (page 73)

Responses will vary but should include facts, examples, and reasons to support main idea.

Editing (page 74)

1. A   **2.** C   **3.** D   **4.** A

UNIT 14

Reading (page 77)

1. B   **3.** A   **5.** A
2. C   **4.** B   **6.** A

7. Responses should include a list of all the examples the narrator gave about being bad at sports coupled with the father's comment that "I just don't think this game is for you."

Composition (page 78)

Responses will vary but should include facts, examples, and reasons that support the main idea.

Editing (page 79)

1. A   **2.** C   **3.** D   **4.** B

UNIT 15

Reading (page 83)

1. B   **3.** A   **5.** D
2. D   **4.** D   **6.** A

7. Responses should list the transition during the Agricultural Revolution from a nomadic society to a society that stayed in one place.
8. Responses should include a listing of the changes that occurred as a result of the revolution chosen.

Composition (page 84)

Responses will vary but should include facts, examples, and reasons to support opinions.

Editing (page 85)

1. C   **2.** A   **3.** B   **4.** A